POCKET
POSITIVES

POCKET

POSITIVES

Compiled by Maggie Pinkney
and Barbara Whiter

The Five Mile Press

The Five Mile Press Pty Ltd
22 Summit Road
Noble Park Victoria 3174
Australia

First published in 1997
Reprinted 1997

This compilation © The Five Mile Press Pty Ltd

Editors: Barbara Whiter and Maggie Pinkney
Cover design: Zöe Murphy
Production: Emma Borghesi
Formatting: Louise Taylor

Printed in Australia by the Australian Print Group

National Library of Australia
Cataloguing-in-Publication data

Includes index.
ISBN 1 87597 141 6

1. Quotations, English. 2. Optimism-Quotations, maxims,
etc. 3. Success-Quotations, maxims, etc.
082

FRONT COVER PHOTOGRAPH
Eagle in Flight
The Australian Picture Library

– Contents –

– Introduction –

We all have emotional highs and lows — it's part of being human. The highs aren't a problem, but the lows can take a hold at times, unless we make a conscious effort to get rid of them. This wonderful anthology of 'pocket positives' — small gems of wisdom — provides the key to shaking off the negatives and focusing on life's positive aspects.

These inspirational quotations are a distillation of the benign and healing thoughts of the world's greatest philosophers, poets and mystics, mixed through with the more pithy observations of actors, humorists, novelists, world leaders and exceptional men and women of many other professions. Wherever possible, the dates, nationality and profession of the person quoted is given.

American actress Helen Hayes acknowledged how much we can gain from the reflections of great minds when she wrote:

> We rely upon the poets, the philosophers, and the playwrights to articulate what most of us can only feel, in joy or sorrow. They illuminate the thoughts for which we only grope; they give us the strength and balm we cannot find in ourselves...the wisdom of acceptance and the resilience to push on.

With more than a thousand quotes to choose from, there's something here to suit every occasion — and every mood. It's worth taking a bit of time out every day to dip into and reflect upon these pocket positives — even if you read only one a day. Anyone who takes to heart the wisdom contained in this book will gain a more enlightened, joyful vision of life. As American golfer Walter Hagen so succinctly put it:

> You're only here for a short visit. Don't hurry. Don't worry. And be sure to smell the flowers along the way.

A

— ABILITY —

What lies behind us, and what lies before us are tiny matters, compared to what lies within us.

Ralph Waldo Emerson (1803-1882)
American essayist, poet and philosopher

When you can do the common things of life in an uncommon way, you will command the attention of the world.

Anonymous

God does not ask about your ability.
He asks about your availability.

Anonymous

— ABUNDANCE —

Life is constantly providing us with new funds,
new resources, even when we are reduced to
immobility. In life's ledger there is no such thing
as frozen assets.

Henry Miller (1892-1971)
American author

The world is so full of a number of things,
I'm sure we should all be as happy as kings.

Robert Louis Stevenson (1850-1894)
Scottish novelist, poet and essayist

Develop interest in life as you see it; in people,
things, literature, music — the world is so rich,
simply throbbing with rich treasures, beautiful
souls and interesting people. Forget yourself.

Henry Miller (1891-1980)
American author

— ACCEPTANCE —

God grant me the serenity to accept the things I cannot change, the courage to change the things I can, and the wisdom to distinguish the one from the other.

Reinhold Niebuhr (1892-1971)
American theologian
(Now the prayer of Alcoholics Anonymous)

Acceptance of others, their looks, their behaviours, their beliefs, brings you an inner peace and tranquillity — instead of anger and resentment.

Anonymous

There is no good in arguing with the inevitable. The only argument available with an east wind is to put on your overcoat.

James Russell Lowell (1819-1891)
American poet and essayist

— ACCOMPLISH —

If you have accomplished all that you have
planned for yourself, you have not
planned enough.

Edward Everett Hale (1822-1909)
American minister and writer

To accomplish great things we must not only act,
but also dream; not only plan, but also believe.

Anatole France (1844-1924)
French writer

What three things do you want to accomplish
this year? Write them down and place them on
your refrigerator for inspiration all year long.

Anonymous

He that is over-cautious will accomplish little.

Friedrich Von Schiller (1759-1805)
German historian and poet

— ACHIEVE —

If you can walk
You can dance.
If you can talk
You can sing.

Traditional Zimbabwe

Only those who dare to fail greatly can ever
achieve greatly.

Robert F. Kennedy (1925-1968)
American senator and attorney-general

To achieve great things we must live as though
we were never going to die.

Luc de Clapiers, Marquis de Vauvenargues (1715-1747)
French moralist and writer

Achieving starts with believing.

Anonymous

— ACTION —

Doing is better than saying.

Proverb

There are risks and costs to a programme of action, but they are far less than the long-range risks and costs of comfortable inaction.

John F. Kennedy (1917-1963)
President of the United States, 1960-1963

A good plan violently executed right now is far better than a perfect plan executed next week.

General George Patton (1885-1945)
American army general

Deliberation is the work of many men. Action, of one alone.

Charles de Gaulle (1890-1970)
French statesman

Do the thing and you will have the power.

Ralph Waldo Emerson (1803-1882)
American essayist, poet and philosopher

Suit the action to the word, the word to the action; with this special observance, that you o'erstep not the modesty of nature.

William Shakespeare (1564-1616)
English playwright and poet

Keep in mind that, even if you're on the right track, you can still be left behind if you just sit there.

Anonymous

After all is said and done, more is said than done.

Anonymous

Do what you can with what you have,
where you are.

Theodore Roosevelt (1858-1919)
President of the United States, 1901-1912

Action makes more fortunes than caution.

Luc de Clapiers, Marquis de Vauvenargues (1715-1747)
French moralist and writer

Footprints on the sands of time are not made
by sitting down.

Proverb

Actions speak louder than words.

Proverb

Never confuse activity with action.

F. Scott Fitzgerald (1896-1940)
American novelist

It is vain to say human beings might be satisfied with tranquillity; they must have action, and they will make it if they can not find it.

Charlotte Brontë (1816-1855)
English novelist

Those who say a thing cannot be done should not stand in the way of those who are doing it.

Anonymous

Boast not of what thou would'st have done,
but do
What then thou would'st.

John Milton (1606-1674)
English poet

The great end of life is not knowledge, but action.

Thomas Fuller (1608-1661)
English divine and historian

— ADVERSITY —

There is no education like adversity.

Benjamin Disraeli, (1804-1881)
English statesman and writer

Turn your stumbling blocks into stepping stones.

Anonymous

He knows not his own strength that hath not
met adversity.

Ben Jonson (1573-1637)
English dramatist

The stars are constantly shining, but often we do
not see them until the dark hours.

Anonymous

What does not destroy me makes me strong.

Friedrich Wilhelm Nietzche (1844-1900)
German philosopher and critic

Adversity is the state in which man most easily
becomes acquainted with himself, being
especially free of admirers then.

Samuel Johnson (1709-1784)
English lexicographer, critic and writer

The way I see it, if you want the rainbow, you
gotta put up with the rain.

Dolly Parton (1946-)
American singer and songwriter

Adversity has the same effect on a man that
severe training has on the pugilist — it reduces
him to his fighting weight.

Josh Billings (1818-1885)
American humorist

— ADVICE —

A good scare is worth more than good advice.

Proverb

No-one wants advice — only corroboration.

John Steinbeck (1902-1968)
American novelist

The way of a fool seems right to him, but a wise
man listens to advice.

Proverbs 12:16

Drink nothing without seeing it;
sign nothing without reading it.

Spanish proverb

— AGEING —

Every man desires to live long, but no man would be old.

Jonathan Swift (1667–1745)
English satirist

Do not go gentle into that good night.
Old age should burn and rage at close of day.

Dylan Thomas (1914–1953)
Welsh poet and writer

He who is of a calm and happy nature will hardly feel the pressure of age.

Plato (c.427–c.347 BC)
Greek philosopher

Many people realise their hearts' desires late in life. Continue learning, never stop striving and keep your curiosity sharp, and you will never become too old to appreciate life.

Anonymous

None are so old as those who have
outlived enthusiasm.

Henry David Thoreau (1817-1862)
American essayist, poet and mystic

It's sad to grow old, but nice to ripen.

Brigitte Bardot (1934-)
French actress

The years between fifty and seventy are the
hardest. You are always being asked to do things,
and you are not yet decrepit enough to turn
them down.

T.S. Eliot (1888-1965)
American-born poet and dramatist

One of the many things nobody ever tells you
about middle age is that it's such a nice change
from being young.

Dorothy Canfield Fisher (1879-1958)
American novelist

I prefer old age to the alternative.

Maurice Chevalier (1888-1972)
French singer and actor

As a white candle
In a holy place,
So is the beauty
Of an old face.

Joseph Campbell (1879-1944)
Irish poet

I will never be an old man. To me, old age is
always 15 years older than I am.

Bernard Baruch (1870-1965)
American financier and presidential adviser

Ageing seems to be the only available way to live
a long life.

Daniel-Francois-Esprit Auber (1782-1871)
French composer

One wastes so much time, one is so prodigal of life, at twenty! Our days of winter count for double. That is the compensation of the old.

George Sand (Amandine Aurore Lucie Dupin)
(1804-1876)
French novelist

Old age is like a plane flying through a storm. Once you're aboard, there's nothing you can do. You can't stop the plane, you can't stop the storm, you can't stop time. So one might as well accept it calmly, wisely.

Golda Meir (1898-1978)
Israeli Prime Minister, 1969-1974

Grey hair is great. Ask anyone who's bald.

Lee Trevino (1937-)
American golfer

No wise man ever wished to be younger.

Jonathan Swift (1667-1745)
English satirist

He who keeps a child in his heart never
grows old.

Anonymous

Old age is like everything else. To make a success
of it, you've got to start young.

Fred Astaire (1899-1987)
American dancer, singer and actor

I look forward to growing old and wise
and audacious.

Glenda Jackson (1937-)
English actor and politician

Youth troubles over eternity, age grasps at a day
and is satisfied to have even the day.

Dame Mary Gilmore (1865-1962)
Australian poet

Age is not important — unless you are a cheese.

Anonymous

On the whole, I take it that middle age is a
happier period than youth.

Alexander Smith (1830-1867)
Scottish poet

To know how to grow old is the master work of
wisdom, and one of the most difficult chapters in
the great art of living.

Henri Frederic Amiel (1821-1881)
Swiss poet and philosopher

The evening of a well-spent life brings its lamps
with it.

Joseph Joubert (1754-1824)
French writer

— AMBITION —

Everybody wants to *be* somebody; nobody wants to *grow*.

Johann Wolfgang von Goethe (1749-1832)
German poet, novelist and playwright

Ah, but a man's reach should exceed his grasp,
Or what's a heaven for?

Robert Browning (1812-1889)
English poet

If you would hit the mark, you must aim a little above it;
Every arrow that flies feels the attraction of earth.

Henry Wadsworth Longfellow (1807-1882)
American poet

27

No bird soars too high if he soars with his own wings.

William Blake (1757-1827)
English poet, artist and mystic

When a man is no longer anxious to do better than well, he is done for.

Benjamin Robert Haydon (1786-1846)
English painter

The rung of a ladder was never meant to rest upon, but only to hold a man's foot long enough to enable him to put the other somewhat higher.

Thomas Henry Huxley (1825-1895)
English biologist

— ANGER —

I was angry with my friend;
I told my wrath, my wrath did end.
I was angry with my foe;
I told it not, my wrath did grow.

William Blake (1757-1827)
English poet, artist and mystic

Man should forget his anger before he lies down
to sleep.

Thomas de Quincey (1785-1859)
English writer

— ANXIETY —

When you don't have any money, the problem is
food. When you have money, it's sex. When you
have both, it's health. If everything is simply jake,
then you're frightened of death.

James Patrick Donleavy (1926-)
Irish-American writer

— APPEARANCE —

Clothes and manners do not make the man; but
when he is made, they greatly improve
his appearance.

Henry Ward Beecher (1813-1887)
American clergyman

There are no ugly women, only lazy ones.

Helena Rubenstein (1870-1965)
American cosmetics manufacturer

Look successful, be successful.

Proverb

Good temper is one of the great preservers of
the features.

William Hazlitt (1778-1830)
English essayist

— APPRECIATION —

We are so often caught up in our destination that we forget to appreciate the journey, especially the goodness of the people we meet on the way. Appreciation is a wonderful feeling, don't overlook it.

Anonymous

— ASPIRATIONS —

Our aspirations are our possibilities.

Samuel Johnson (1709-1784)
English lexicographer, critic and writer

We can always redeem the man who aspires and tries.

Johann Wolfgang von Goethe (1749-1832)
German poet

— ATTITUDE —

Attitudes are more important than facts.

Norman Vincent Peale (1898-1993)
American writer and minister

A relaxed attitude lengthens a man's life.

Anonymous

We are all in the gutter, but some of us are looking at the stars.

Oscar Wilde (1854-1900)
Irish poet, wit and dramatist

Nothing is good or bad, but thinking makes it so.

William Shakespeare (1564-1616)
English dramatist and poet

Take the attitude of a student. Never be too big to ask questions. Never know too much to learn something new.

Og Mandino (1923-)
American author

The greatest revolution of our generation is the discovery that human beings, by changing the inner attitudes of their minds, can change the outer aspects of their lives.

William James (1842-1910)
American psychologist and philosopher

If a man does not keep pace with his companions, perhaps it is because he hears a different drummer. Let him step to the music which he hears, however measured or far away.

Henry David Thoreau (1817-1862)
American essayist, poet and mystic

B

— BEAUTY —

People are like stained-glass windows. They sparkle and shine when the sun is out, but when the darkness sets in, their true beauty is revealed only if there is a light from within.

Elisabeth Kubler-Ross (1926-)
Swiss-born American psychiatrist

To look *almost* pretty is an acquisition of higher delight to a girl who has been looking plain for the first fifteen years of her life than a beauty from her cradle can ever receive.

Jane Austen (1775-1817)
English novelist

It is very necessary to have makers of beauty left in a world seemingly bent on making the most evil ugliness.

Vita Sackville-West (1892-1962)
English writer, poet and renowned gardener

Character contributes to beauty. It fortifies a woman as her youth fades. A mode of conduct, a standard of courage, discipline, fortitude and integrity can do a great deal to make a woman beautiful.

Jacqueline Bisset (1946-)
English actress

Though we travel the world over to find the beautiful, we must carry it with us or we find it not.

Ralph Waldo Emerson (1803-1882)
American essayist, poet and philosopher

Things are beautiful if you love them.

Jean Anouilh (1910-1987)
French dramatist

— BEGINNING —

'Tis always morning somewhere in the world.

Richard Henry Horne (1803-1884)
English writer

✱

Whatever you can do or dream you can, begin it.
Boldness has genius, power and magic in it.

Johann Wolfgang von Goethe (1749-1832)
German poet, novelist and playwright

✱

A journey of a thousand miles must begin with a
single step.

Lao-Tze (c.604 BC)
Chinese philosopher and founder of Taoism

✱

All glory comes from daring to begin.

Eugene F. Ware (1841-1911)
American laywyer and verse-writer

— BELIEF —

The secret of making something work in your lives is first of all, the deep desire to make it work: then the faith and belief that it can work: then to hold that clear definite vision in your consciousness and see it working out step by step, without one thought of doubt or disbelief.

Eileen Caddy
Co-founder of The Findhorn Foundation, Scotland

We are what we believe we are.

Benjamin Nathan Cardozo (1870-1938)
American jurist

The thing always happens that you really believe in; and the belief in a thing makes it happen.

Frank Lloyd Wright (1869-1959)
American architect

Believe nothing of what you hear, and only half
of what you see.

Proverb

Believe that life is worth living, and your belief
will help create the fact.

William James (1842-1910)
American psychologist and philosopher

Whether you believe you can do a thing or
believe you can't, you are right.

Henry Ford (1863-1947)
American motor car manufacturer

Belief consists in accepting the affirmations of the
soul; unbelief in denying them.

Ralph Waldo Emerson (1803-1882)
American essayist, poet and philosopher

— BEST —

One does not know — cannot know — the best
that is in one.

Friedrich Wilhelm Nietzsche (1844-1900)
German philosopher and critic

It is a funny thing about life; if you refuse to
accept anything but the best, you very often
get it.

W. Somerset Maugham (1874-1965)
English writer

I am easily satisfied with the very best.

Sir Winston Churchill (1874-1965)
English statesman

There is a better way to do it; find it.

Thomas A. Edison (1847-1931)
American inventor

Believe in the best, think your best, study your best, have a goal for your best, never be satisfied with less than your best, try your best, and in the long run things will turn out for the best.

Henry Ford (1863-1947)
American motor car manufacturer

Good, better, best,
May you never rest,
Until your good is better,
And your better best.

Anonymous

Only mediocrity is always at its best.

Max Beerbohm (1872-1956)
English writer and caricaturist

Don't let the best you have done so far be the standard for the rest of your life.

Gustavus F. Swift (1839-1903)
American meat industry magnate

— BIG —

Do not be afraid to take a big step if one is
required. You can't cross a chasm in two
small jumps.

David Lloyd George (1863-1945)
British Prime Minister, 1916-1922

Think big.

Anonymous

— BIRTHDAYS —

Her birthdays were always important to her, for
being a born lover of life, she would always keep
the day of her entrance into it as a very great
festival indeed.

Elizabeth Goudge (1900-1984)
English author

— BLESSED —

'Tis being and doing and having that make
All the pleasures and pains of which
mankind partake;
To be what God pleases, to do a man's best,
And to have a good heart, is the way to be blest.

Lord Byron (1788-1824)
English poet

Blest, who can unconcern'dly find
Hours, days, and years, slide soft away
In health of body, peace of mind,
Quiet by day,
Sound sleep by night; study and ease
Together mix'd; sweet recreation,
And innocence, which most does please
With meditation.
Thus let me live, unseen unknown;
Thus unlamented let me die;
Steal from the world, and not a stone
Tell where I lie.

Alexander Pope (1688-1744)
English poet

— BLESSING —

May you have food and raiment,
A soft pillow for your head.
May you be half an hour in heaven,
Before the devil knows you're dead.

Traditional Irish

Go, little book, and wish to all
Flowers in the garden, meat in the hall,
A bin of wine, a spice of wit,
A house with lawns enclosing it,
A living river by the door,
A nightingale in the sycamore.

Robert Louis Stevenson (1850-1894)
Scottish novelist, poet and essayist

Now may every living thing, young or old, weak
or strong, living near or far, known or unknown,
living or departed or yet unborn, may every
living thing be full of bliss.

Buddha (5th century BC)
The founder of Buddhism

— BOOKS —

How many a man has dated a new era in his life
from the reading of a book?

Henry David Thoreau (1817-1862)
American essayist, poet and mystic

Make books your companions; let your
bookshelves be your gardens: bask in their
beauty, gather their fruit, pluck their roses, take
their spices and myrrh.

Samuel ben Judah ibn Tibbon (1150-1230)
French-Jewish translator and physician

A good book is the best of friends, the same today
and forever.

Martin Farquhar Tupper (1810-1889)
English writer

It is impossible to mentally or socially enslave a Bible-reading people. The principles of the Bible are the groundwork of human freedom.

Horace Greeley (1811-1872)
American journalist

The New Testament is the very best book that was ever or ever will be known in the world.

Charles Dickens (1812-1870)
English novelist

All that mankind has done, thought, or been is lying in magic preservation in the pages of books.

Thomas Carlyle (1795-1881)
Scottish essayist, historian and philosopher

Books are the quietest and most constant of friends; they are the most accessible and wisest of counsellors, and the most patient of teachers.

Charles W. Eliot (1834-1926)
English educator

We rely upon the poets, the philosophers, and the playwrights to articulate what most of us can only feel, in joy or sorrow. They illuminate the thoughts for which we only grope; they give us the strength and balm we cannot find in ourselves. Whenever I feel my courage wavering I rush to them. They give me the wisdom of acceptance, the will and resilience to push on.

Helen Hayes (1900-1993)
American actress

Literature is my Utopia. Here I am not disenfranchised. No barrier of the sense shuts me out from the sweet, gracious discourses of my book friends. They talk to me without embarrassment or awkwardness.

Helen Keller (1880-1966)
Deaf and blind American lecturer, writer and scholar

— BRAIN —

The chief purpose of the body is to carry the
brain around.

Thomas A. Edison (1847-1931)
American inventor

I not only use all the brains I have, but all
I can borrow.

Woodrow Wilson (1856-1925)
President of the United States, 1913-1921

— BRAVERY —

Bravery is being the only one who knows
you're afraid.

Franklin P. Jones (1832-1902)
American capitalist and politician

— BRIGHT SIDE —

No one ever hurt their eyesight by looking at the
bright side of life.

Anonymous

If you can't see the bright side, polish the
dull side.

Anonymous

It is worth a thousand pounds a year to have the
habit of looking on the bright side of things.

Samuel Johnson (1709-1784)
English lexicographer, critic and writer

— BUSINESS —

The secret of business is to know something that
nobody else knows.

Aristotle Socrates Onassis (1906-1975)
Greek shipping magnate

Live together like brothers, but do business
like strangers.

Anonymous

Beware of all enterprises that require
new clothes.

Henry David Thoreau (1817-1862)
American essayist, poet and mystic

Customer service is not a business slogan but a
religion unto itself.

Japanese business philosophy

The happiest time in any man's life is when he is in red-hot pursuit of a dollar, with a reasonable prospect of overtaking it.

Josh Billings (1818-1885)
American humorist

It is not the employer who pays wages — he only handles the money. It is the product that pays wages.

Henry Ford (1863-1947)
American motor car manufacturer

Business should be fun. Without fun, people are left wearing emotional raincoats most of their working lives. Building fun into business is vital; it brings life into our daily being. Fun is a powerful motive for most of our activities and should be a direct path of our livelihood. We should not relegate it to something we buy after work with money we earn.

Michael Phillips (1943 -)
American movie producer

C

— CAREERS —

The best careers advice to give to the young is 'Find out what you like doing best and get someone to pay you for doing it'.

Katharine Whitehorn (1926-)
English newspaper columnist

Never turn a job down because you think it's too small; you don't know where it could lead.

Julia Morgan (1872-1957)
American architect

Plough deep while sluggards sleep.

Benjamin Franklin (1706-1790)
American statesman and philosopher

— CHANGE —

Things do not change: we change.

Henry David Thoreau (1817-1862)
American essayist and poet

You can't step into the same river twice.

Heraclitus (c.535-c.475 BC)
Greek philospher

If you don't like it, change it. If you don't want to change it, it can't be that bad.

Anonymous

Change is a part of every life. Resisting is often as futile as it is frustrating.

Anonymous

Everything flows and nothing stays.

Heraclitus (c.535–c.475 BC)
Greek philospher

Determination, patience and courage are the only things needed to improve any situation. And, if you want a situation changed badly enough, you will find these three things.

Anonymous

We shrink from change; yet is there anything that can come into being without it? What does Nature hold dearer, or more proper to herself? Could you have a hot bath unless the firewood underwent some change...Is it possible for any useful thing to be achieved without change? Do you not see, then, that change in yourself is of the same order, and no less necessary to Nature?

Marcus Aurelius (121–180 AD)
Roman emperor and philosopher

— CHAOS —

Chaos often breeds life, when order breeds habit.

Henry Brooks Adams (1838-1918)
American historian, journalist and teacher

I say to you: one must have chaos in oneself in
order to give birth to a dancing star.

Friedrich Wilhelm Nietzsche (1844-1900)
German philosopher and critic

Out of chaos comes order.

Anonymous

A degree of chaos can be liberating to the
creative spirit.

Anonymous

— CHARACTER —

Character consists of what you do on the third
and fourth tries.

James A. Michener (1907-)
American writer

Talent develops in quiet places, character in the
full current of human life.

Johann Wolfgang von Goethe (1749-1832)
German poet, novelist and playwright

In everyone there is something precious, found in
no-one else; so honour each man for what is
hidden within him — for what he alone has, and
none of his fellows.

Hasidic saying

Surely the world we live in is but the world that
lives in us.

Daisy Bates (1836-1915)
Australian social worker

The tree which moves some to tears of joy is, in the eye of others, only a green thing which stands in the way. As a man is, so he sees.

William Blake (1757-1827)
English poet, artist and mystic

In matters of style, swim with the current; in matters of principle, stand like a rock.

Thomas Jefferson (1743-1826)
President of the United States, 1801-1809

A man should endeavour to be as pliant as a reed, yet as hard as cedar wood.

The Talmud

— CHARITY —

With malice toward none, with charity for all.

Abraham Lincoln (1809-1865)
President of the United States, 1861-1865

— CHOICE —

Only she who says
She did not choose, is the loser in the end.

Adrienne Rich (1929-)
American writer

The absence of alternatives clears the
mind marvellously.

Henry Alfred Kissinger (1923-)
German-American statesman and university professor

You can be whatever type of person you choose
to be. Your habits, your behaviours, your
responses, are all your choice.

Anonymous

Happiness or unhappiness is often a matter
of choice.

Anonymous

Only by keeping the past alive in our memories
can we choose what to discard and what to retain
in our present way of life.

Lady (Phyllis Dorothy) Cilento (1894-1987)
Doctor, medical journalist and nutritionist

Every tomorrow has two handles. You can take
hold of the handle of anxiety or the handle of
enthusiasm. Upon your choice so will be the day.

Anonymous

Two roads diverged into a wood, and I —
I took the one less travelled by,
And that has made all the difference.

Robert Frost (1875-1963)
American poet

When you have to make a choice and you don't
make it, that itself is a choice.

William James (1842-1910)
American psychologist and philosopher

— COMFORT —

Whenever I have found that I have blundered or
that my work has been imperfect, and when I
have been contemptuously criticised and even
when I have been overpraised, so that I have felt
mortified, it has been my greatest comfort to say
hundreds of times to myself that 'I have worked
as hard and as well as I could, and no man can
do more than this.'

Charles Darwin (1809-1882)
English naturalist

And this for comfort thou must know:
Times that are ill won't still be so;
Clouds will not ever pour down rain;
A sullen day will clear again.

Robert Herrick (1591-1674)
English poet

— COMMITMENT —

We know what happens to people who stay in the
middle of the road. They get run over.

Aneurin Bevan (1897-1960)
British Labour politician

In for a penny, in for a pound.

Proverb

I have nothing to offer but blood, toil, tears
and sweat.

Sir Winston Churchill (1874-1965)
English statesman

If a job is worth doing, it's worth doing properly.

Proverb

— COMPROMISE —

Better bend than break.

Scottish proverb

You cannot shake hands with a clenched fist.

Indira Gandhi (1917-1984)
Indian stateswoman and Prime Minister

— COMPUNCTION —

The beginning of compunction is the beginning
of a new life.

George Eliot (Mary Ann Evans) (1819-1880)
English novelist

— CONCENTRATION —

Concentration is my motto. First honesty, then
industry, then concentration.

Andrew Carnegie (1835-1919)
Scottish-American industrialist and philanthropist

The shortest way to do many things is to do only
one thing at once.

Samuel Smiles (1812-1904)
Scottish author and social reformer

— CONFIDENCE —

Confidence is realising that although you aren't
the best at something, you still enjoy doing it.

Anonymous

Confidence is the memory of past success.

Anonymous

— CONSCIENCE —

Conscience: something that feels terrible when everything else feels swell.

Anonymous, from *Reader's Digest*, 1949

Conscience is a cur that will let you get past it, but that you cannot stop from barking.

Anonymous

A man's vanity tells him what is honour; a man's conscience what is justice.

Walter Savage Landor (1775-1864)
English poet and writer

— CONSEQUENCES —

In nature there are neither rewards nor punishments — there are consequences.

Robert Green Ingersoll (1833-1899)
American agnostic

— CONSTANCY —

Plus ça change, plus c'est la même chose. (The more things change, the more they stay the same.)

Alphonse Karr (1808-1890)
French writer

— CONTENTMENT —

Contentment is accepting the world as an imperfect place.

Anonymous

Contentment is not an emotion of incredible highs, because incredible highs always guarantee incredible lows. Contentment is satisfaction over a life that's steady, but fulfilling all the same.

Anonymous

— COURAGE —

Come to the edge, he said.
They said: We are afraid.
Come to the edge, he said.
They came.
He pushed them, and they flew...

Guillaume Apollinaire (1880-1918)
French poet

There is only one courage and that is the courage
to let go of the past, not to collect it, not to
accumulate it, not to cling to it. We all cling to
the past, and because we cling to the past we
become unavailable to the present.

Bhagwan Shree Rajneesh
Indian spiritual cult leader

Courage is what it takes to stand up and speak;
courage is also what it takes to sit down
and listen.

Anonymous

Courage is resistance to fear, mastery of fear, not absence of fear.

Mark Twain (1835-1910)
American writer and humorist

No one has looked back sadly on a life full of experiences, but many look back wishing they had had the courage to do more.

Anonymous

Courage is reckoned the greatest of all virtues, because, unless a man has that virtue, he has no security for preserving any other.

Samuel Johnson (1709-1784)
English lexicographer, critic and writer

What the hell — you might be right, you might be wrong — but don't just avoid.

Katharine Hepburn (1909-)
American actor

You gain strength, courage and confidence by every experience in which you really stop to look fear in the face...You must do the thing you cannot do.

Eleanor Roosevelt (1884-1962)
First Lady of the United States, 1933-1945

If the creator had a purpose in equipping us with a neck, he surely meant us to stick it out.

Arthur Koestler (1905-1983)
Hungarian-born writer

What a new face courage puts on everything.

Ralph Waldo Emerson (1803-1883)
American essayist, poet and philosopher

A stout heart breaks bad luck.

Miguel de Cervantes (1547-1616)
Spanish writer

Presence of mind and courage in distress,
Are more than brave armies to procure success.

John Dryden (1631-1700)
English poet and dramatist

Any coward can fight a battle when he's sure of
winning, but give me the man who has pluck to
fight when he's sure of losing.

George Eliot (Mary Ann Evans) (1819-1880)
English novelist

Courage is the price that Life exacts for
granting peace.

Amelia Earhart (1898-1937)
American aviator

Man cannot discover new oceans until he has
courage to lose sight of the shore.

Anonymous

If one is forever cautious, can one remain a
human being?

Alexander Solzhenitsyn (1918-)
Russian writer

— *COURTESY* —

Civility costs nothing.

Proverb

Good manners are made up of petty sacrifices.

Ralph Waldo Emerson (1803-1882)
American essayist, poet and philosopher

Forget the etiquette books. The whole point of
good manners is to put the other person at ease.

Anonymous

— CREATIVITY —

Emptiness is a symptom that you are not living creatively. You either have no goal that is important enough to you, or you are not using your talents and efforts in striving toward an important goal.

Maxwell Maltz
American motivational writer

Creative minds have always been known to survive any kind of bad training.

Anna Freud (1895-1982)
Austrian psychoanalyst

When in doubt, make a fool of yourself. There is a microscopically thin line between being brilliantly creative and acting like the most gigantic idiot on earth. So what the hell, leap.

Cynthia Heimel
American feminist writer (from Village Voice, *1983)*

— CRITICISM —

To avoid criticism, do nothing, say nothing,
be nothing.

Elbert Hubbard (1856-1915)
American writer

Great Spirit, grant that I may not criticize my
neighbour until I have walked a mile in
his moccasins.

American Indian prayer

If you judge people, you have no time to
love them.

Mother Teresa of Calcutta (1910-)
Yugoslav-born missionary

A little self-criticism is as beneficial as too much
is harmful.

Anonymous

If you hear that someone is speaking ill of you, instead of trying to defend yourself, you should say: 'He obviously does not know me very well, since there are so many other faults he could have mentioned.'

Epictetus (c.60-110 AD)
Stoic philosopher

He has the right to criticise, who has a heart to help.

Abraham Lincoln (1809-1865)
President of United States, 1861-1865

— CURIOSITY —

Curiosity is a gift, a capacity of pleasure in knowing, which if you destroy, you make yourselves cold and dull.

John Ruskin (1819-1900)
English author and art critic

A sense of curiosity is nature's original school of education.

Smiley Blanton (1882-1966)
American musician

The important thing is not to stop questioning.

Albert Einstein (1879-1955)
German-born American physicist

Whoever retains the natural curiosity of childhood is never bored or dull.

Anonymous

D

— DEATH —

Death is nothing at all; it does not count. I have only slipped away into the next room.

Canon Henry Scott-Holland (1847-1918)
British cleric

Do not stand at my grave and weep;
I am not there. I do not sleep.
I am a thousand winds that blow.
I am the diamond glints on snow.
I am the sunlight on ripened grain.
I am the gentle autumn's rain.
When you awaken in the morning's hush,
I am the swift uplifting rush
Of quiet birds in circled flight.
I am the soft stars that shine at night.
Do not stand at my grave and cry;
I am not there. I did not die.

Anonymous

It matters not how a man dies, but how he lives.
The act of dying is not of importance, it lasts so
short a time.

Samuel Johnson (1709-1784)
English lexicographer, critic and writer

It is better to die on your feet than live on
your knees.

Dolores Ibarruri (1895-1989)
Spanish communist leader and orator

Death can show us the way, for when we know
and understand completely that our time on this
earth is limited, and that we have no way of
knowing when it will be over, then we must live
each day as if it were the only one we had.

Elisabeth Kubler-Ross (1926-)
Swiss-born American psychiatrist

To fear death, gentlemen, is nothing other than to think oneself wise when one is not; for it is to think one knows what one does not know. No man knows whether death may not even turn out to be the greatest of blessings for a human being; and yet people fear it as if they knew for certain that it is the greatest of evils.

Socrates (c.469-399 BC)
Greek philosopher

As a goldsmith, taking a piece of gold transforms it into another newer and more beautiful form, even so this self, casting off this body and dissolving its ignorance, makes for itself another newer and more beautiful form.

Brhadaranyaka IV:43-4

Death is but crossing the world, as friends do the seas; they live in one another still.

William Penn (1644-1718)
English Quaker and founder of Pennsylvania, USA

What will survive of us is love.

Philip Larkin (1922-1985)
English poet

Thinking about death...produces love for life.
When we are familiar with death, we accept
each week, each day, as a gift. Only if we are able
thus to accept life — bit by bit — does it
become precious.

Albert Schweitzer (1875-1965)
Alsatian medical missionary

The years seem to rush by now, and I think of
death as a fast approaching end of a journey —
double and treble the reason for loving as well as
working while it is day.

George Eliot (Mary Ann Evans) (1819-1880)
English novelist

Death is the final stage of growth in this life.
There is no total death. Only the body dies. The
self or spirit, or whatever you may wish to label
it, is eternal.

Elisabeth Kubler-Ross (1926-)
Swiss-born American psychiatrist

To die completely, a person must not only forget
but be forgotten, and he who is not forgotten is
not dead.

Samuel Butler (1835-1902)
English writer and satirist

When we truly love, it is never lost. It is only
after death that the depth of the bond is truly felt,
and our loved one becomes more a part of us
than was possible in life.

Oriental tradition

— DECISIONS —

You don't drown by falling in the water. You drown by staying there.

Anonymous

No trumpets sound when the important decisions of our life are made. Destiny is made known silently.

Agnes de Mille (1908-)
American choreographer

Whenever you see a successful business, someone once made a courageous decision.

Peter Drucker (1909-)
American management consultant

— DEEDS —

Our grand business in life is not to see what lies
dimly at a distance, but to do what lies clearly
at hand.

Thomas Carlyle (1795-1881)
Scottish essayist, historian and philosopher

A man can only do what he can do. But if he does
that each day he can sleep at night and do it
again the next day.

Albert Schweitzer (1875-1965)
Alsatian medical missionary

By his deeds we know a man.

African proverb

What counts in life is not what you say but what
you do.

Anonymous

A deed knocks first at Thought
And then — it knocks at Will —
That is the manufacturing spot.

Emily Dickinson (1830-1886)
American poet

✴

Our deeds travel with us from afar, and what we
have been makes us what we are.

George Eliot (Mary Ann Evans) (1819-1880)
English novelist

✴

The shortest answer is doing.

English Proverb

✴

Every thought I have imprisioned in expression I
must free by my deeds.

Kahlil Gibran (1883-1931)
Lebanese writer, artist and mystic

— DEFEAT —

Do not be afraid of defeat. You are never so near
victory as when defeated in a good cause.

Henry Ward Beecher (1813-1887)
American clergyman

— DELIGHT —

Among the mind's powers is one that comes of
itself to many children and artists. It need not be
lost, to the end of his days, by anyone who has
ever had it. This is the power of taking delight in
a thing, or rather in anything, not as a means to
some other end, but just because it is what it is. A
child in the full health of his mind will put his
hand flat on the summer lawn, feel it, and give a
little shiver of private glee at the elastic firmness
of the globe.

Charles Edward Montague (1867-1928)
English novelist and essayist

— DESIRE —

Lord, grant that I may always desire more than I can accomplish.

Michelangelo (1474-1564)
Italian sculptor, painter and poet

Desires are only the lack of something: and those who have the greatest desires are in a worse condition than those who have none, or very slight ones.

Plato (c.427-347 BC)
Greek philosopher

Desire is the very essence of man.

Benedict Spinoza (1632-1677)
Dutch philosopher

— DESPAIR —

Despair doubles our strength.

French proverb

It is always darkest just before the day dawneth.

Thomas Fuller (1608-1661)
English divine and historian

When we are flat on our backs there is no way to look but up.

Roger W. Babson (1875-1967)
American economist

In the midst of winter, I finally learned that there was in me an invincible summer.

Albert Camus (1913-1960)
French writer

— DESTINY —

To live content with small means; to seek
elegance rather than luxury, and refinement
rather than fashion; to be worthy, not
respectable, and wealthy, not rich; to study
hard, think quietly, talk gently, act frankly; to
listen to stars and birds, to babes and sages, with
open heart; to bear all cheerfully, do all bravely,
await occasions, hurry never. In a word to let the
spiritual, unbidden and unconscious, grow up
through the common. This is to be
my symphony.

William Ellery Channing (1780-1842)
American minister

If thou follow thy star, thou canst not fail of a
glorious haven.

Dante Alighieri (1265-1321)
Italian poet, statesman and diplomat

Destiny: a tyrant's excuse for crime and a fool's excuse for failure.

Ambrose Bierce (1842-1911)
American journalist

Destiny is not a matter of chance, it is a matter of choice.

William Jennings Bryan (1860-1925)
American lawyer and politician

Everything that happens happens as it should, and if you observe carefully, you will find this to be so.

Marcus Aurelius (121-180 AD)
Roman emperor and philosopher

We are not creatures of circumstance; we are creators of circumstance.

Benjamin Disraeli (1804-1881)
English statesman and writer

— DIFFICULTY —

All things are difficult before they are easy.

Thomas Fuller (1608-1661)
English divine and historian

The hill, though high, I covet to ascend;
The difficulty will not offend,
For I perceive the way to life lies here.
Come, pluck up heart, let's neither faint nor fear;
Better, though difficult, the right way to go,
Than wrong, though easy,
Where the end is woe.

John Bunyan (1628-1688)
English writer and moralist

Keep the faculty of effort alive in you by a little
gratuitous exercise every day. That is be
systematically heroic in little unnecessary points,
do every day or two something for no other
reason than its difficulty.

William James (1842-1910)
American psychologist and philosopher

— DIRECTION —

I can't change the direction of the wind. But I can
adjust my sails.

Anonymous

Determine on some course, more than a wild
exposure to each chance.

William Shakespeare (1564-1616)
English playwright and poet

The thing has already taken form in my mind
before I start it. The first attempts are absolutely
unbearable. I say this because I want you to know
that if you see something worthwhile in what I
am doing, it is not by accident but
because of real direction and purpose.

Vincent van Gogh (1853-1890)
Dutch post-impressionist painter

— DISCIPLINE —

Discipline is the soul of an army. It makes small numbers formidable, procures success to the weak, and esteem to all.

George Washington (1732-1799)
First President of the United States, 1789-1797

— DISCOVERY —

The real voyage of discovery consists not in seeking new landscapes but in having new eyes.

Marcel Proust (1871-1922)
French novelist

Discovery consists of seeing what everybody has seen and thinking what nobody has thought.

Albert Szent-Györgyi (1893-unknown)
Hungarian-born American biochemist

— DREAMS —

Dreams don't have to come true by age 20, 30 or 40: they often occur long past when you thought possible.

Anonymous

All big men are dreamers. They see things in the soft haze of a spring day or in the red fire of a long winter's evening. Some of us let great dreams die, but others nourish and protect them, nurse them through bad days till they bring them to the sunshine and light which comes always to those who sincerely hope that their dreams will come true.

Woodrow Wilson (1856-1925)
President of the United States, 1913-1921

Some men see things as they are and say 'Why?' I dream things that never were, and say, 'Why not?'

George Bernard Shaw (1856-1950)
Irish dramatist, essayist and critic

Go confidently in the direction of your dreams!
Live the life you've imagined.

Henry David Thoreau (1817-1862)
American essayist, poet and mystic

If you have built castles in the air, your work
need not be lost; that is where they should be.
Now put the foundations under them.

Henry David Thoreau (1817-1862)
American essayist, poet and mystic

Take your dream, attach it to a star and never
lose it. If you lose it...you've lost your
enthusiasm; you've settled for something less.
This will never do. Fight like hell for your
dream and get it.

Guru RHH

If there were dreams to sell,
What would you buy?
Some cost a passing-bell;
Some a light sigh.

Thomas Lovell Beddoes (1803-1849)
English poet and physiologist

Those who dream by day are cognizant of many
things which escape those who dream only
by night.

Edgar Allan Poe (1809-1849)
American poet and writer

Dreams are the touchstones of our characters.

Henry David Thoreau (1817-1862)
American essayist, poet and mystic

★

The future belongs to those who believe in the
beauty of their dreams.

Eleanor Roosevelt (1884-1962)
First Lady of the United States, 1933-1945

★

Who looks outside dreams; who looks
inside wakes.

Carl Jung (1875-1961)
Swiss psychiatrist

All men dream, but not equally. Those who
dream by night in the dusty recesses of their
minds wake in the day to find that it was vanity:
but the dreamers of the day are dangerous men,
for they may act their dream with open eyes, to
make it possible.

T.E. Lawrence (Lawrence of Arabia) (1888-1935)
English soldier and writer

My dreams were all my own; I accounted for
them to nobody; they were my refuge when
annoyed — my dearest pleasure when free.

Mary Shelley (1797-1851)
English author

Learning to understand our dreams is a matter of learning to understand our heart's language.

Anne Faraday (1935-   )
American psychologist and dream researcher

An uninterpreted dream is like an unopened letter.

Jewish proverb

— *DURABILITY* —

The more I study the world, the more I am convinced of the inability of brute force to create anything durable.

Napoleon Bonaparte I (1769-1821)
French emperor

E

— EDUCATION —

Education is simply the soul of a society as it passes from one generation to another.

G.K. Chesterton (1874-1936)
English writer

If you educate a man you educate a person, but if you educate a woman you educate a family.

Ruby Manikan (20th century)
Indian church leader

— ENDURANCE —

Nothing happens to any man that he is not
formed by nature to bear.

Marcus Aurelius (121-180 BC)
Roman emperor and philosopher

Endure, and keep yourself for days of happiness

Virgil (70-19 BC)
Roman poet

We could never learn to be brave and patient if
there were only joy in the world.

Helen Keller (1880-1968)
Deaf and blind American lecturer, writer and scholar

No pain, no palm; no thorns, no throne; no gall,
no glory; no cross, no crown.

William Penn (1644-1718)
English Quaker and founder of Pennsylvania, USA

— ENEMIES —

Beware of no man more than yourself; we carry
our worst enemies within us.

Charles Haddon Spurgeon (1834-1892)
English clergyman

— ENERGY —

If an unusual necessity forces us onward, a
surprising thing occurs. The fatigue gets worse
up to a certain point, when, gradually or
suddenly, it passes away and we are fresher than
before! We have evidently tapped a new level of
energy. There may be layer after layer of this
experience, a third and fourth wind. We find
amounts of ease and power that we never
dreamed ourselves to own, sources of strength
habitually not taxed, because habitually we never
push through the obstruction of fatigue.

William James (1842-1910)
American psychologist and philosopher

— ENJOYMENT —

At the judgement day a man will be called to account for all the good things he might have enjoyed and did not enjoy.

Jewish proverb

He neither drank, smoked, nor rode a bicycle. Living frugally, saving his money, he died early, surrounded by greedy relatives. It was a great lesson to me.

John Barrymore (1882-1942)
American actor

— ENTHUSIASM —

Nothing great was ever achieved
without enthusiasm.

Ralph Waldo Emerson (1803-1882)
American essayist, poet and philosopher

None so old as those who have
outlived enthusiasm.

Henry David Thoreau (1817-1862)
American poet, essayist and mystic

If you are not getting as much from life as you
want to, then examine the state of
your enthusiasm.

Norman Vincent Peale (1898-1993)
American writer and minister

The person who loves always
becomes enthusiastic.

Norman Vincent Peale (1898-1993)
American writer and minister

Act enthusiastic and you become enthusiastic.

Dale Carnegie (1888-1955)
American author and lecturer

You can do anything if you have
enthusiasm...Enthusiasm is at the bottom of all
progress. With it, there is accomplishment.
Without it, there are only alibis.

Henry Ford (1863-1947)
American motor car manufacturer

No man who is enthusiastic about his work has
anything to fear from life.

Samuel Goldwyn (1882-1974)
American film producer

Do not be afraid of enthusiasm. You need it. You can do nothing effectively without it.

Francois Pierre Guillaume Guizot (1787-1874)
French historian and statesman

The love of life is necessary to the vigorous prosecution of any undertaking.

Samuel Johnson (1709-1784)
English lexicographer, critic and writer

We act as though comfort and luxury were the chief requirements of life, when all that we need to make us really happy is something to be enthusiastic about.

Charles Kingsley (1819-1875)
English writer and clergyman

— EXCELLENCE —

Excellence is to do a common thing in an
uncommon way.

Booker Taliaferio Washington (1856-1915)
American teacher, writer and speaker

— EXCUSES —

He that is good at making excuses is seldom good
at anything else.

Benjamin Franklin (1706-1790)
American statesman and philospher

The trick is not how much pain you feel — but
how much joy you feel. Any idiot can feel pain.
Life is full of excuses to feel pain, excuses not to
live, excuses, excuses, excuses.

Erica Jong (1942-)
American novelist and poet

— EXPERIENCE —

Experience is not what happens to a man. It is what a man does with what happens to him.

Aldous Huxley (1894-1963)
English novelist and essayist

Nothing ever becomes real till it is experienced. Even a proverb is no proverb to you till your life has illustrated it.

John Keats (1795-1821)
English poet

And other's follies teach us not,
Nor much their wisdom teaches,
And most, of sterling worth, is what
Our own experience teaches.

Alfred, Lord Tennyson (1809-1892)
English poet

Experience is the name everyone gives to
their mistakes.

Oscar Wilde (1854-1900)
Irish poet, wit and dramatist

Experience is a hard teacher because she gives
the test first, the lesson afterwards.

Vernon Sanders Law

The art of living is the art of using experience —
your own and other people's.

Herbert Louis Samuel (1870-1963)
British politician and administrator

Experience isn't interesting till it begins to repeat
itself — in fact, till it does that, it hardly
is experience.

Elizabeth Bowen (1899-1973)
Irish novelist

A moment's insight is sometimes worth a
life's experience.

Oliver Wendell Holmes (1809-1894)
American writer

Experience is one thing you can't get for nothing.

Oscar Wilde (1854-1900)
Irish poet, wit and dramatist

– *EXTRAORDINARY* –

The difference between ordinary and
extraordinary is that little extra.

Anonymous

F

— FAILURE —

When we begin to take our failures
non-seriously, it means we are ceasing to be
afraid of them. It is of immense importance to
learn to laugh at ourselves.

Katherine Mansfield (1888-1923)
New Zealand author

If at first you don't succeed you're running
about average.

Margaret H. Alderson *(1959-)*
Journalist

A failure is a man who has blundered, but is not
able to cash in on the experience.

Elbert Hubbard (1856-1915)
American writer

He who never fails will never grow rich.

Charles Haddon Spurgeon (1834-1892)
English clergyman

We are all of us failures — at least the best of
us are.

J.M. Barrie (1860-1937)
Scottish writer

He's no failure. He's not dead yet.

Gwilym Lloyd George (1894-1967)
Welsh politician

Say not that she did well or ill,
Only 'She did her best'.

Dinah Maria Craik (1826-1887)
English novelist and poet

If men could regard the events of their lives with more open minds they would frequently discover that they did not really desire the things they failed to obtain.

André Maurois (1885-1967)
French writer

We learn wisdom from failure much more than success. We often discover what we WILL do, by finding out what we will NOT do.

Samuel Smiles (1812-1904)
Scottish author and social reformer

There is only one real failure in life that is possible and that is, not to be true to the best one knows.

Frederic Farrer (1831-1903)
English clergyman and writer

— FAITH —

Be still, sad heart! and cease repining;
Behind the clouds is the sun still shining;
Thy fate is the common fate of all,
Into each life some rain must fall.

Henry Wadsworth Longfellow (1807-1882)
American poet

They can because they think they can.

Virgil (70-19 BC)
Roman poet

Without winter, there can be no spring.
Without mistakes, there can be no learning.
Without doubts, there can be no faith.
Without fears, there can be no courage.
My mistakes, my fears and my doubts are my
path to wisdom, faith and courage.

Anonymous

I feel no need for any other faith than my faith in human beings.

Pearl S. Buck (1892-1973)
American novelist

In the midst of outer dangers I have felt an inner calm and known resources of strength that only God could give. In many instances I have felt the power of God transforming the fatigue of despair into the buoyancy of hope. I am convinced that the universe is under the control of a loving purpose and that in the struggle for righteousness man has cosmic companionship. Behind the harsh appearances of the world there is a benign power.

Martin Luther King (1929-1968)
American black civil-rights leader

Proof is the last thing looked for by a truly religious mind which feels the imaginative fitness of its faith.

George Santayana (1863-1952)
Spanish-American philosopher and poet

Dame Edith Sitwell, when asked why she had come to faith, said she had looked at the pattern of a frosted flower on a window-pane, she had studied shells, feathers, petals and grasses, and she knew without doubt there must be a cause...

Quoted in *Christian Poetry*

He who sees the Infinite in all things sees God.

William Blake (1757-1827)
English poet, artist and mystic

I believe in God and in nature and in the triumph of good over evil.

Johann Wolfgang von Goethe (1749-1832)
German poet, novelist and playwright

If you have abandoned one faith, do not abandon all faith. There is always an alternative to the faith we lose. Or could it be the same thing under another mask?

Graham Greene (1904-1991)
English novelist

— FATE —

Whatever fate befalls you, do not give way to great rejoicing, or great lamentation...All things are full of change, and your fortunes may turn at any moment.

Arthur Schopenhauer (1788-1860)
Philosopher

Lots of folks confuse bad management with destiny.

Frank McKinney Hubbard (1868-1930)

I do not believe in a fate that falls on men however they act; but I do believe in a fate that falls on them unless they act.

G.K. Chesterton (1874-1936)
English writer

— FAULTS —

When you have faults, do not fear to
abandon them.

Confucius (551-479 BC)
Chinese philosopher

We all have faults. It's important to recognise
your own, but to try and turn a blind eye to the
faults of others.

Anonymous

Love your enemies, for they tell you your faults.

Benjamin Franklin (1706-1790)
American statesman and philosopher

— FEAR —

Fear is never a reason for quitting: it is only
an excuse.

Norman Vincent Peale (1898-1993)
American writer and minister

To fear love is to fear life, and those who fear life
are already three parts dead.

Bertrand Russell (1872-1970)
English philosopher and mathematician

Do the thing you fear and the death of fear
is certain.

Ralph Waldo Emerson (1803-1882)
American essayist, poet and philosopher

There is no fear in love; but perfect love casteth
out fear: because fear hath torment. He that
feareth is not made perfect in love.

1 John 4:18

Nothing in life is to be feared. It is only to
be understood.

Marie Curie (1867-1934)
French physicist

Let me assert my firm belief that the only things
we have to fear is fear itself.

Franklin D. Roosevelt (1882-1945)
President of the United States, 1932-1945

To conquer fear is the beginning of wisdom, in
the pursuit of truth as in the endeavour after a
worthy manner of life.

Bertrand Russell (1872-1970)
English philosopher and mathematician

Considering how dangerous everything is
nothing is really very frightening.

Gertrude Stein (1874-1946)
American author

Of all the liars in the world, sometimes the worst are your own fears.

Rudyard Kipling (1865-1936)
English poet and author

When I became ill, the years of pain and confusion loomed up like some primitive monster of the deep. I had to face the monster or drown. There were many nights when I thought I was going under for the last time. I lived in fear of dying. The strange paradox is that by confronting my fear of death, I found myself and created a new life.

Lucia Capacchione
American art therapist and pioneer in inner healing

Carry your own lantern and you need not fear the dark.

Leo Rosten's Treasury of Jewish Quotations

— FORGIVENESS —

Forgive your enemies, but never forget
their names.

John F. Kennedy (1917-1963)
President of the United States, 1961-1963

Lift up your eyes and look on one another in
innocence born of complete forgiveness of each
other's illusions.

A Course in Miracles

The forgiving state of mind is a magnetic power
for attracting good. No good thing can be
withheld from the forgiving state of mind.

Catherine Ponder
American motivational writer

To err is human, to forgive, divine.

Alexander Pope (1688-1744)
English poet

The reason to forgive is for your own sake. For
our own health Because beyond that point
needed for healing, if we hold onto our anger, we
stop growing and our souls begin to shrivel.

M. Scott Peck (1936-)
American psychiatrist and writer

One forgives as much as one loves.

Francois, Duc de La Rochefoucauld (1616-1680)
French writer

Sometimes the hardest person to forgive is
yourself. But we shouldn't be harder on ourselves
than we would be on others.

Anonymous

— FREEDOM —

Once freedom lights its beacon in a man's heart,
the gods are powerless against him.

Jean-Paul Sartre (1905-1980)
French writer

I disapprove of what you say, but I will defend to
the death your right to say it.

Voltaire (1694-1778)
French author

The moment the slave resolves that he will no
longer be a slave, his fetters fall. He frees himself
and shows the way to others. Freedom and
slavery are mental states.

Mahatma Gandhi (1869-1948)
Indian leader, moral teacher and reformer

★

Freedom is the right to tell people what they do not want to hear.

George Orwell (1903-1950)
English novelist

Man is free at the moment he wishes to be.

Voltaire (1694-1778)
French writer

You only have power over people so long as you don't take everything away from them. But when you've robbed a man of everything he's no longer in your power — he's free again.

Alexander Solzhenitsyn (1918-)
Russian writer

Freedom's just another word for nothing left to lose.

Kris Kristofferson (1936-)
American actor and folk singer

The most beautiful thing in the world is freedom
of speech.

Diogenes (412?-323 BC)
Greek philosopher

Liberty, when it begins to take root, is a plant of
rapid growth.

George Washington (1732-1799)
First President of the United States, 1789-1797

Liberty means responsibility. That is why most
dread it.

George Bernard Shaw (1856-1950)
Irish dramatist, essayist and critic

The love of liberty is the love of others.
The love of power is the love of ourselves.

William Hazlitt (1778-1830)
English essayist

— FRIENDS —

Your friend is the man who knows all about you,
and still likes you.

Elbert Hubbard (1856-1915)
American writer

The only way to have a friend is to be one.

Ralph Waldo Emerson (1803-1882)
American essayist, poet and philosopher

Friendship is always a sweet responsibility, never
an opportunity.

Kahlil Gibran (1883-1931)
Lebanese poet, writer, artist and mystic

So long as we are loved by others I should say
that we are almost indispensable; and no man is
useless while he has a friend.

Robert Louis Stevenson (1850-1894)
Scottish novelist, poet and essayist

Slender at first, they quickly gather force,
Growing in richness as they run their course;
Once started, they do not turn back again:
Rivers, and years, and friendships with good men.

Sanskrit poem

Don't sacrifice your life to work and ideals. The
most important things in life are human
relations. I found that out too late.

Katharine Susannah Prichard (1883-1969)
Australian author

Am I not destroying my enemies when I make
friends of them?

Abraham Lincoln (1809-1865)
President of the United States, 1861-1865

A man who turns his back on his friends soon
finds himself facing a very small audience.

Dick Powell (1904-1963)
American actor

No man is wise enough by himself.

Titus Maccius Plautus (250-184 BC)
Roman poet and comic playwright

Forsake not an old friend; for the new is not
comparable to him: a new friend is as new wine;
when it is old, thou shalt drink it with pleasure.

Ecclesiastes

Instead of loving your enemies treat your friends
a little better.

E.W. Howe (1853-1937)
American novelist

Friendship consists in forgetting what one gives,
and remembering what one receives.

Alexandré Dumas (1803-1870)
French novelist

He that is a friend to himself, know; he is a friend to all.

Montaigne (1533-1592)
French essayist

Animals are such agreeable friends — they ask no questions, they pass no criticisms.

George Eliot (Mary Ann Evans) 1819-1880
English novelist

Be a friend to thyself and others will too.

Thomas Fuller (1608-1661)
English divine and historian

What is a friend? A single soul dwelling in two bodies.

Aristotle (384-322 BC)
Greek philosopher

The thread of our life would be dark,
Heaven knows!
If it were not with friendship and love
intertwined.

Thomas Moore (1779-1852)
Irish poet

Where there are friends, there is wealth.

Titus Maccius Plautus (250-184 BC)
Roman poet and comic playwright

They are rich who have true friends.

Thomas Fuller (1608-1661)
English divine and historian

Friendship is a sheltering tree.

Samuel Taylor Coleridge (1772-1834)
English poet

Friendship is the gift of the gods, and the most precious boon to man.

Benjamin Disraeli (1804-1881)
English statesman and author

You can always tell a real friend: when you've made a fool of yourself he doesn't feel you've done a permanent job.

Laurence J. Peter (1918-)
Canadian writer

The light of friendship is like the light of phosphorus, even plainest when all around is dark.

Grace Crowell (1877-1969)
American poet

— FULFILMENT —

Fulfilment is deciding what you want out of life,
and working towards it. Fulfilment is not merely
the reaching of a specific destination.

Anonymous

Fulfilment is reaching your own expectations, not
the expectations of others.

Anonymous

It is never too late to be what you might
have been.

George Eliot (Mary Ann Evans)
(1819-1880)
English novelist

— FUTURE —

I am not interested in the past. I am interested in the future, for that is where I expect to spend the rest of my life.

Charles Franklin Kettering (1876-1958)
American engineer and inventor

Future — that period of time in which our affairs prosper, our friends are true and our happiness is assured.

Ambrose Bierce (1842-1914)
American writer

What are you looking forward to in the next year? The next ten years? Isn't it exciting to imagine all the possibilities the future holds?

Anonymous

Never let the future disturb you. You will meet it,
if you have to, with the same weapons of reason
which today arm you against the present.

Marcus Aurelius (121-180 AD)
Roman emperor and philosopher

The best thing about the future is that it comes
only one day at a time.

Abraham Lincoln (1809-1865)
President of United States, (1861-1865)

To most of us the future seems unsure; but then it
always has been, and we who have seen great
changes must have great hopes.

John Masefield (1878-1967)
English poet

G

— GARDENS —

Who loves a garden still his Eden keeps,
Perennial pleasures, plants and wholesome
harvest reaps.

Amos Bronson Alcott (1799-1888)
American teacher and philosopher

Yes, in the poor man's garden grow
Far more than herbs and flowers —
Kind thoughts, contentments, peace of mind,
And joy for weary hours.

Mary Howitt (1799-1888)
English author

He who has roses in his garden also has roses in
his heart.

Anonymous

I scorn the doubts and cares that hurt
The world and all its mockeries,
My only care is now to squirt
The ferns among my rockeries.
In early youth and later life
I've seen an up and seen a down,
And now I have a loving wife
To help me peg verbena down.

In peace and quiet pass our days,
With nought to vex our craniums,
Our middle beds are all ablaze
With red and white geraniums.

Let him who'd have the peace he needs
Give all his worldly mumming up,
Then dig a garden, plant the seeds,
And watch the product coming up.

George R. Sims (1847-1922)
English poet

★

One is nearer God's Heart in a garden,
Than anywhere else on earth.

Dorothy Frances Gurney (1858-1932)
English poet

★

— GENIUS —

Genius is one per cent inspiration and
ninety-nine per cent perspiration.

Thomas A. Edison (1847-1931)
American inventor

One is not born a genius, one becomes a genius.

Simone de Beauvoir (1908-1986)
French writer

Genius is nothing but labour and diligence.

William Hogarth (1697-1764)
English painter and political caricaturist

To believe your own thought, to believe that what
is true for you in your private heart is true for all
men — that is genius.

Ralph Waldo Emerson (1803-1882)
American essayist, poet and philosopher

— GIFTS —

You are surrounded by gifts every living moment
of every day. Let yourself feel appreciation for
their presence in your life and take the time to
acknowledge their splendour.

Lon G. Nungesser
Writer

Earth's crammed with heaven,
And every common bush afire with God.

Elizabeth Barrett Browning (1806-1861)
English poet

O gift of God! a perfect day,
Whereon shall no man work but play,
Whereon it is enough for me
Not to be doing but to be.

Henry Wadsworth Longfellow (1807-1882)
American poet

— GIVING —

You give but little when you give of your
possessions. It is when you give of yourself
that you truly give.

Kahlil Gibran (1883-1931)
Lebanese poet, writer, artist and mystic

The only gift is a portion of thyself.

Ralph Waldo Emerson (1803-1882)
American essayist, poet and philosopher

The manner of giving is worth more than
the gift.

Pierre Corneille (1606-1684)
French dramatist

Every man according as he purposeth in his
heart, so let him give; not grudgingly, or out of
necessity: for God loveth a cheerful giver.

Corinthians 9:7

— GOALS —

You have to know what you want to get. But
when you know that, let it take you. And if it
seems to take you off the track, don't hold back,
because perhaps that is instinctively where you
want to be. And if you hold back and try to be
always where you have been before, you
will go dry.

Gertrude Stein (1874-1946)
American writer

One can never consent to creep when one feels
an impulse to soar.

Helen Keller (1880-1968)
Deaf and blind American lecturer, writer and scholar

Shoot for the moon. Even if you miss it you will
land among the stars.

Les (Lester Louis) Brown (1928-)
Journalist

All successful people have a goal. No one can get anywhere unless he knows where he wants to go and what he wants to be or do.

Norman Vincent Peale (1898-1993)
American writer and minister

A man without a purpose is like a ship without a rudder.

Thomas Carlyle (1795-1881)
Scottish essayist, historian and philosopher

The world stands aside for he who knows where he is going.

Proverb

The significance of a man is not in what he attains, but rather in what he longs to attain.

Kahil Gibran (1883-1931)
Lebanese writer, artist and mystic

We're all born under the same sky, but we don't all have the same horizon.

Konrad Adenauer (1876-1967)
German lawyer and statesman

Knowing your destination is half the journey.

Anonymous

Once you say you're going to settle for second, that's what happens to you in life, I find.

John F. Kennedy (1917-1963)
President of United States, 1960-1963

— GOOD —

Do all the good you can,
By all the means you can,
In all the ways you can,
In all the places you can,
At all the times you can,
To all the people you can,
As long as ever you can.

John Wesley (1703-1791)
English evangelist and founder of Methodism

Set your sights high, the higher the better. Expect the most wonderful things to happen, not in the future but right now. Realise that nothing is too good. Allow absolutely nothing to hamper you or hold you up in any way.

Eileen Caddy
Co-founder of The Findhorn Foundation, Scotland

What is a weed? A plant whose virtues have not been discovered.

Ralph Waldo Emerson (1803-1882)
American poet and essayist

Goodness does not more certainly make men happy than happiness makes them good.

Walter Savage Landor (1775-1864)
English poet and writer

Nothing can harm a good man, either in life or after death.

Socrates (469-399 BC)
Greek philosopher

What is beautiful is good, and who is good will soon also be beautiful.

Sappho (died 610 BC)
Greek lyric poet

— GREATNESS —

There is a great man, who makes every man feel
small. But the real great man is the man who
makes every man feel great.

G.K. Chesterton (1874-1936)
English author

It's great to be great, but it's greater to
be human.

Will Rogers (1879-1935)
American actor and humorist

For the courage of greatness is adventurous and
knows not withdrawing,
But grasps the nettle danger, with resolute hands,
And ever again
Gathers security from the sting of pain.

Vera Brittain (1893-1970)
English author and poet

Lives of great men all remind us
We can make our lives sublime,
And, departing leave behind us
Footprints on the sands of time.

Henry Wadsworth Longfellow (1807-1882)
American poet

We are all worms, but I do believe that I am a
glow-worm.

Sir Winston Churchill (1874-1965)
English statesman

One can build the Empire State Building,
discipline the Prussian army, make a state
hierarchy mightier than God, yet fail to overcome
the unaccountable superiority of certain
human beings.

Alexander Solzhenitsyn (1918-)
Russian writer

— GROWTH —

The great law of culture is: Let each become all
that he was created capable of being.

Thomas Carlyle (1795-1881)
Scottish essayist, historian and philosopher

My business is not to remake myself,
But make the absolute best of what God made.

Robert Browning (1812-1889)
English poet

Love not what you are but what you
may become.

Miguel de Cervantes (1547-1616)
Spanish author

Moments of guilt, moments of contrition,
moments when we are lacking in self-esteem,
moments when we are bearing the trial of being
displeasing to ourselves, are essential to
our growth.

M. Scott Peck (1936-)
American psychiatrist and writer

Be not afraid of growing slowly. Be afraid of
standing still.

Chinese proverb

Examine myself as I may, I can no longer find the
slightest trace of the anxious, agitated individual
of those years, so discontented with herself, so
out of patience with others.

George Sand (Amandine Aurora Lucie Dupin)
(1804-1876)
French novelist

Large streams from little fountains flow,
Tall oaks from little acorns grow.

David Everett (1770-1813)
English poet and writer

The creation of a thousand forests is
in one acorn.

Ralph Waldo Emerson (1803-1882)
American essayist, poet and philosopher

Real development is not leaving things behind, as
on a road, but drawing life from them,
as on a root.

G.K. Chesterton (1874-1936)
English writer

H

— HABIT —

Habit is a great deadener.

Samuel Beckett (1906-1989)
Irish novelist and dramatist

The chains of habit are too weak to be felt until they are too strong to be broken.

Samuel Johnson (1709-1784)
English lexicographer, critic and writer

Habit is habit, and not to be flung out the window by man, but coaxed downstairs, a step at a time.

Mark Twain (1835-1910)
American writer and humorist

— HAPPINESS —

One joy scatters a hundred griefs.

Chinese proverb

One is happy as a result of one's own efforts,
once one knows the necessary ingredients of
happiness — simple tastes, a certain degree of
courage, self-denial to a point, love of work, and
above all, a clear conscience. Happiness is no
vague dream.

George Sand (Amandine Aurore Lucie Dupin)
(1804-1876)
French novelist

It is impossible for a man to be made happy by
putting him in a happy place, unless he be first in
a happy state.

Benjamin Whichcote (1609-1683)
English philosopher and theologian

The supreme happiness of life is the conviction that we are loved; loved for ourselves, or rather, loved in spite of ourselves.

Victor Hugo (1802-1885)
French poet and author

Happiness is as a butterfly which, when pursued, is always beyond our grasp, but which, if you will sit down quietly, may alight upon you.

Nathaniel Hawthorne (1804-1864)
American novelist and short story writer

All happiness depends on a leisurely breakfast.

John Gunter (1938-)
English designer

We spend so much time yearning for that special item that will finally make us happy, that we don't take the time to look around and discover that we already are.

Anonymous

Happiness is a mystery like religion, and should never be rationalised.

G.K. Chesteron (1874-1936)
English author

A lifetime of happiness! No man alive could bear it: it would be hell on earth.

George Bernard Shaw (1856-1950)
Irish dramatist, essayist and critic

Happiness lies in the joy of achievement and the thrill of creative effort.

Franklin D. Roosevelt (1882-1945)
President of the United States, 1933-1945

Action may not always bring happiness, but there is no happiness without action.

Benjamin Disraeli (1804-1881)
English statesman and writer

Knowledge of what is possible is the beginning
of happiness.

George Santayana (1863-1952)
Spanish-American philosopher and poet

Happiness doesn't depend on the actual number
of blessings we manage to scratch from life, only
our attitude towards them.

Alexander Solzhenitsyn (1918-)
Russian writer

When a small child...I thought that success
spelled happiness. I was wrong. Happiness is like
a butterfly which appears and delights us for one
brief moment, but soon flits away.

Anna Pavlova (1881-1931)
Russian ballet dancer

Happiness in this world, when it comes, comes incidentally. Make it the object of pursuit, and it leads us a wild-goose chase, and is never attained.

Nathaniel Hawthorne (1804-1864)
American novelist and short story writer

The happiest people seem to be those who are producing something; the bored people are those who are consuming much and producing nothing.

William Inge (1860-1954)
English prelate and author

To be without some of the things you want is an indispensable part of happiness.

Bertrand Russell (1872-1970)
English philosopher and mathematician

There is no duty we so much underestimate as the duty of being happy. Being happy we sow anonymous benefits upon the world.

Robert Louis Stevenson (1850-1894)
Scottish novelist, poet and essayist

The best way to future happiness is to be as happy as is rightfully possible today.

Charles W. Eliot (1834-1926)
English educator

Most happy is he who is entirely self-reliant, and who centres all his requirements on himself.

Marcus Tullius Cicero (106-43 BC)
Roman orator, statesman and writer

The happiness of life is made up of minute fractions. The little soon forgotten charities of a kiss or smile, a kind look, a hearfelt compliment — countless infinitesimals of pleasurable and genial feelings.

Samuel Taylor Coleridge (1772-1834)
English poet

A man is happy so long as he chooses to be happy.

Alexander Solzhenitsyn (1918-)
Russian writer

Man's life is happy mainly because he is always expecting that it will soon be so.

Edgar Allen Poe (1809-1849)
American poet and writer

There is only one happiness in life, to love and to be loved...

George Sand (Amandine Aurore Lucie Dupin)
(1804-1876)
French novelist

— HATRED —

It's a sign of your own worth sometimes if you
are hated by the right people.

Miles (Stella Maria) Franklin (1879-1954)
Australian writer

Hatred and bitterness can never cure the disease
of fear; only love can do that. Hatred paralyses
life; love harmonises it. Hatred darkens life; love
illumines it.

Martin Luther King (1929-1968)
American black civil-rights leader

Hatred rarely does any harm to its object. It is the
hater who suffers.

Lord Beaverbrook (1879-1964)
Canadian-born newspaper proprietor

— HEALTH —

Health and cheerfulness mutually beget
each other.

Joseph Addison (1672-1719)
English essayist

✳

To wish to be well is a part of becoming well.

Seneca (4 BC-65 AD)
Roman philosopher and statesman

✳

To get the body in tone, get the mind in tune.

Zachary T. Bercovitz (1895-1984)
American doctor and writer

✳

Look to your health; and if you have it, praise
God, and value it next to a good conscience; for
health is the second blessing that we mortals are
capable of; a blessing that money can not buy.

Isaak Walton (1593-1683)
English writer

— HEART —

The heart of the wise, like a mirror, should reflect all objects, without being sullied by any.

Confucius (551-479 BC)
Chinese philosopher

Keep a green tree in your heart and perhaps a singing bird will come.

Chinese proverb

The best exercise for the heart is to bend over backwards for someone else.

Anonymous

I love thee for a heart that's kind.
Not for the knowledge in thy mind.

W.H. Davies (1871-1940)
Welsh poet

— HEAVEN —

Heaven means to be at one with God.

Confucius (551-479 BC)
Chinese philosopher

As much of heaven is visible as we have eyes
to see.

William Winter (1836-1917)
American dramatic critic and poet

The Way of Heaven has no favourites. It is always
with the good man.

Lao-Tze (c.604 BC)
Chinese philosopher and founder of Taoism

Earth has no sorrow that Heaven cannot heal.

Thomas Moore (1779-1852)
Irish poet

— HELP —

If a friend is in trouble, don't annoy him by
asking him if there's anything you can do. Think
of something appropriate and do it.

E.W. Howe (1853-1937)
American writer

No-one is useless in the world who lightens the
burden of it for anyone else.

Charles Dickens (1812-1870)
English author

Many hands make light work.

Proverb

Troubles shared are troubles halved.

Proverb

— HOME —

A man travels the world over in search of what
he needs and returns home to find it.

George Moore (1852-1933)
Irish writer and art critic

No place is more delightful than one's
own fireside.

Marcus Tullius Cicero (106-43 BC)
Roman orator, statesman and writer

But what on earth is half so dear — so longed for
— as the hearth of home?

Emily Brontë (1818-1848)
English poet and novelist

Whom God loves, his house is sweet to him.

Miguel de Cervantes (1547-1616)
Spanish writer

A comfortable home is a great source of happiness. It ranks immediately after health and a good conscience.

Sydney Smith (1771-1845)
English essayist, clergyman and writer

My kitchen is a mystical place, a kind of temple for me. It is a place where the surfaces seem to have significance, where the sounds and odors carry meaning that transfers from the past and bridges to the future.

Pearl Bailey (1918-1986)
American singer

— HONESTY —

Being entirely honest with oneself is a good exercise.

Sigmund Freud (1856-1939)
Austrian founder of psychoanalysis

— HOPE —

There are no hopeless situations; there are only men who have grown hopeless about them.

Clare Booth Luce (1903-1987)
American playwright

Do not fear to hope...
Each time we smell the autumn's dying scent,
We know that primrose time will come again.

Samuel Taylor Coleridge (1772-1834)
English poet

We should not let our fears hold us back from pursuing our hopes.

John F. Kennedy (1917-1963)
President of the United States, 1960-1963

Great hopes make great men.

Thomas Fuller (1608-1661)
English divine and historian

We must accept finite disappointment, but we must never lose infinite hope.

Martin Luther King (1929-1968)
American black civil-rights leader

Hope is itself a species of happiness and, perhaps, the chief happiness which this world affords.

Samuel Johnson (1709-1784)
English lexicographer, critic and writer

For what human ill does not dawn seem to be an alleviation?

Thornton Wilder (1897-1975)
American writer

Everything that is done in the world is done by hope.

Martin Luther (1483-1546)
German religious reformer

— HUMOUR —

Humour is mankind's greatest blessing.

Mark Twain (1835-1910)
American writer and humorist

Total absence of humour renders life impossible.

Colette (1873-1954)
French novelist

Everything is funny, as long as it's happening to somebody else.

Will Rogers (1879-1935)
American actor and humorist

He deserves paradise who makes his companions laugh.

The Koran

I

– IDEAS –

Greater than the tread of mighty armies is an
idea whose time has come.

Victor Hugo (1802-1885)
French poet and author

A crank is a man with a new idea — until it
catches on.

Mark Twain (1835-1910)
American writer and humorist

What was once thought can never be unthought.

Friedrich Durrenmatt (1921-)
Swiss writer

If you don't follow through on your creative ideas, someone else will pick them up and use them. When you get an idea of this sort, you should jump in with both feet, not just stick your toe in the water... Be daring, be fearless, and don't be afraid that somebody is going to criticize you or laugh at you. If your ego is not involved no-one can hurt you.

Guru RHH

A stand can be made against invasion by an army; no stand can be made against invasion by an idea.

Victor Hugo (1802-1885)
French writer

— *IGNORANCE* —

To be conscious that you are ignorant is a great step to knowledge.

Benjamin Disraeli (1804-1881)
English statesman and writer

— IMAGINATION —

What is now proved was once only imagined.

William Blake (1757-1827)
English poet, artist and mystic

Man's mind, once stretched by a new idea, never
regains its original dimension.

Oliver Wendell Holmes (1809-1894)
American writer

Imagination is more important than knowledge.

Albert Einstein (1879-1955)
German-born physicist

This world is but canvas to our imaginations.

Henry David Thoreau (1817-1862)
American essayist, poet and mystic

Imagination is the highest kite one can fly.

Lauren Bacall (1924-)
American actress

Imagination, industry and intelligence — 'the three I's' — are all indispensable to the actress, but of these three the greatest is, without any doubt, imagination.

Ellen Terry (1848-1928)
English actress

There are no rules of architecture for a castle in the clouds.

G.K. Chesterton (1874-1936)
English critic, novelist and poet

— IMPERFECTION —

No one should abandon duties because he see
defects in them. Every action, every activity, is
surrounded by defects as a fire is surrounded
by smoke.

Bhagavad Gita

— IMPRESSION —

You never get a second chance to make a good
first impression.

Anonymous

Every man is a hero and an oracle to somebody,
and to that person, whatever he says has an
enhanced value.

Ralph Waldo Emerson (1803-1882)
American essayist, poet and philosopher

— INDEPENDENCE —

Depend not on another, but lean instead on
thyself...True happiness is born of self-reliance.

The Laws of Manu, Hindu teachings

It's easy to be independent when you've got
money. But to be independent when you haven't
got a thing — that's the Lord's test.

Mahalia Jackson (1911-1972)
American spirituals singer

The strongest man in the world is he who
stands alone.

Henrik Ibsen (1828-1906)
Norwegian dramatist

Follow your own bent, no matter what
people say.

Karl Marx (1818-1883)
German philosopher

— INDIVIDUALITY —

Conformity is one of the most fundamental
dishonesties of all. When we reject our
specialness, water down our God~given
individuality and uniqueness, we begin to lose
our freedom. The conformist is in no way a free
man. He has to follow the herd.

Norman Vincent Peale (1898-1993)
American writer and minister

Every individual has a place to fill in the world,
and is important, in some respect, whether he
chooses to be or not.

Nathaniel Hawthorne (1804-1864)
American novelist

— INTEGRITY —

If you don't stand for something...you'll fall
for anything.

Anonymous

Integrity without knowledge is weak and useless,
and knowledge without integrity is dangerous
and dreadful.

Samuel Johnson (1709-1784)
British lexicographer, critic and writer

My strength is as the strength of ten,
Because my heart is pure.

Alfred, Lord Tennyson (1809-1892)
English poet

This above all — to thine own self be true,
And it must follow, as night follows day,
Thou canst not then be false to any man.

William Shakespeare (1564-1616)
English playwright and poet

— INTUITION —

Intelligence highly awakened is intuition, which
is the only true guide in life.

Jiddu Krishnamurti (1895-1986)
Indian theosophist

We belittle an intuition, calling it only a hunch,
and therefore not be taken too seriously. I
encourage you to take your hunches and
intuitions very seriously. They contain some of
your highest, most profound insights
and wisdom.

Lucia Capacchione
American art therapist and pioneer in inner healing

Intuition is a truth that arrives in the
mind unbidden.

Anonymous

J

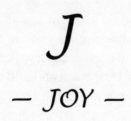

— JOY —

May your joys be as deep as the ocean, your
sorrows as light as its foam.

Anonymous

The life without festivals is a long road without
an inn.

Democritus (c.460 BC)
Greek philosopher

Joy exists only in self-acceptance. Seek perfect
acceptance, not a perfect life.

Anonymous

Joy is not in things; it is in us.

Richard Wagner (1813-1883)
German composer

Joy, Lady, is the spirit and the power,
Which wedding nature gives to us in dower,
A new earth and new heaven,
Undreamt of by the sensual and the proud —
Joy is the sweet voice, joy the luminous cloud —
We in ourselves rejoice.

Samuel Taylor Coleridge (1772-1834)
English poet

Joy is one of nature's greatest medicines. Joy is
always healthy. A pleasant state of mind tends to
bring abnormal conditions back to normal.

Catherine Ponder
American motivational writer

Taking joy in life is a woman's best cosmetic.

Rosalind Russell (1911-1976)
American actress

The more joy we have, the more nearly perfect
we are.

Benedict Spinoza (1632-1677)
Dutch philosopher

— JUDGEMENT —

Each person you meet is in a specific stage of their life, a stage you may have passed or not yet reached. Judging them by your standards and experience is therefore not only unfair, but could lead to unnecessary anger and frustration.

Anonymous

— JUSTICE —

Though the sword of justice is sharp, it will not slay the innocent.

Chinese proverb

Justice is truth in action.

Benjamin Disraeli (1804-1881)
English statesman and writer

K

— KINDNESS —

Recompense injury with justice, and recompense
kindness with kindness.

Confucius (551-479 BC)
Chinese philosopher

No act of kindness, no matter how small, is
ever wasted.

Aesop (c. 550 BC)
Greek fable-maker

My religion is very simple — my religion
is kindness.

Dalai Lama (1935-)
Tibetan spiritual leader

Kindness is a language which the blind can see
and the deaf can hear.

Anonymous

Think deeply; speak gently; love much; laugh
often; work hard; give freely; pay promptly;
be kind.

Anonymous

I expect to pass through life but once. If,
therefore, there be any kindness I can show, or
any good thing I can do to any fellow being, let
me do it now, for I shall not pass this way again.

William Penn (1644-1718)
English Quaker and founder of Pennsylvania, USA

Little deeds of kindness,
Little words of love,
Help to make earth happy
Like the heaven above.

Julia Fletcher Carney (1823-1908)
American teacher

We cannot always return an act of kindness to
the person who bestowed it, but we can pay back
the debt by helping others.

Anonymous

Wise words often fall on barren ground; but a
kind word is never thrown away.

Arthur Helps (1813-1875)
English historian

Kindness which is bestowed on the good
is never lost.

Plato (426-c.347 BC)
Greek philosopher

The heart benevolent and kind
The most resembles God.

Robert Burns (1759-1796)
Scottish poet

The best portion of a good man's life,
His little, nameless, unremembered acts of
kindness and love.

William Wordsworth (1770-1850)
English poet

Getting money is not all a man's business: to
cultivate kindness is a valuable part of the
business of life.

Samuel Johnson (1709-1784)
English lexicographer, critic and writer

One kind word can warm three winter months.

Japanese saying

— KNOWLEDGE —

I thank Thee, Lord, for knowing me better than I
know myself,
And for letting me know myself better than
others know me.
I pray Thee then, make me better than they
suppose,
And forgive me for what they do not know.

Abu Bekr (573-634)
Father-in-law of Mohammed, his follower and successor

We do not know one-millionth of one per cent
about anything.

Thomas A. Edison (1847-1931)
American inventor

I am sufficiently proud of my knowing
something to be modest about my not knowing
everything.

Vladimir Nabokov (1899-1977)
Russian-born American author

A good listener is not only popular everywhere,
but after a while he gets to know something.

Wilson Mizner (1876-1933)
American humorist

Knowledge and timber shouldn't be much used
till they are seasoned.

Oliver Wendell Holmes (1809-1894)
American writer and physician

Knowledge is the action of the soul.

Ben Jonson (1573-1637)
English dramatist

Knowledge advances by steps, and not by leaps.

Thomas Macaulay (1800-1859)
English historian and statesman

An investment in knowledge always pays the best interest.

Benjamin Franklin (1706-1790)
American statesman and philosopher

What we want is to see the child in pursuit of knowledge, and not knowledge in pursuit of the child.

George Bernard Shaw (1856-1950)
Irish dramatist, essayist and critic

It is the greatest nuisance that knowledge can only be acquired by hard work.

W. Somerset Maugham (1874-1965)
English writer

Knowledge is power.

Francis Bacon (1561-1626)
English philosopher

★

L

— LAUGHTER —

Laughter is the sensation of feeling good all over, and showing it principally in one place.

Josh Billings (1818-1885)
American humorist

Laughter is sunshine in a house.

William Makepeace Thackeray (1811-1863)
English author

A complete revaluation takes place in your physical and mental being when you've laughed and had some fun.

Catherine Ponder
American motivational writer

Laughter has something in it in common with the
ancient winds of faith and inspiration; it
unfreezes pride and unwinds secrecy; it makes
men forget themselves in the presence of
something greater than themselves; something
that they cannot resist.

G.K. Chesterton (1874-1936)
English critic, novelist and poet

The most wasted of all days is that on which one
has not laughed.

Nicolas Chamfort (1741-94)
French writer

Laugh and the world laughs with you;
Weep, and you weep alone.

Ella Wheeler Wilcox (1850-1919)
American poet

It's impossible to speak highly enough of the
virtues, the dangers and the power of
shared laughter.

Françoise Sagan (1935-)
French novelist

We are all here for a spell. Get all the good
laughs you can.

Will Rogers (1879-1935)
American actor and humorist

Among those whom I like or admire, I can find
no common denominator, but among those I love,
I can: all of them make me laugh.

W.H. Auden (1907-1973)
English poet and essayist

He who laughs, lasts.

Anonymous

— LAZINESS —

For one person who dreams of making fifty thousand pounds, a hundred people dream of being left fifty thousand pounds.

A.A. Milne (1882-1956)
English writer

It is the doom of laziness and gluttony to be inactive without ease, and drowsy without tranquillity.

Samuel Johnson (1709-1784)
English lexicographer, critic and writer

Indolence is a delightful but distressing state. We must be doing something to be happy.

William Hazlitt (1778-1830)
English essayist

— LEADERSHIP —

I learned that a great leader is a man who has the ability to get other people to do what they don't want to do and like it.

Harry S. Truman (1884-1972)
President of the United States, 1945-1952

Leadership: the art of getting someone else to do something you want done because he wants to do it.

Dwight D. Eisenhower (1890-1969)
President of the United States, 1953-1961

The great difference between the real leader and the pretender is — that the one sees into the future, while the other regards only the present; the one lives by the day, and acts upon expediency; the other acts on enduring principles and for immortality.

Edmund Burke (1729-1797)
British politician and writer

— LEARNING —

Blessed are those who listen, for they shall learn.

Anonymous

No man e'er found a happy life by chance,
Or yawned it into being with a wish.
An art it is, and must be learnt; and learnt
With unremitting effort, or be lost.

Edward Young (1683-1765)
English poet

Have you learned lessons only of those who
admired you, and were tender with you, and
stood aside for you? Have you not learned great
lessons from those who braced themselves
against you, and disputed the passage with you?

Walt Whitman (1819-1891)
American poet

That is what learning is. You suddenly understand something you've understood all your life, but in a new way.

Doris Lessing (1919-)
English novelist

What we have to learn to do, we learn by doing.

Aristotle (384-322 BC)
Greek philosopher

Natural abilities are like natural plants; they need pruning by study.

Francis Bacon (1561-1626)
English philosopher

Learning makes a man fit company for himself.

Thomas Fuller (1608-1661)
English divine and historian

— LIFE —

To live long, live slowly.

Marcus Tullius Cicero (106-43 BC)
Roman orator, statesman and writer

Decide carefully, exactly what you want in life,
then work like mad to make sure you get it!

Hector Crawford (1913-1991)
Australian television program-maker

Life is either a daring adventure or nothing.

Helen Keller (1880-1968)
Deaf and blind American lecturer, writer and scholar.

Live every day as though it's your last. One day
you'll get it right!

Zig Ziglar
American writer and motivational speaker

★

Life is what happens to you while you're busy making other plans.

John Lennon (1940-1980)
English singer and songwriter

When I hear somebody sigh, 'Life is hard,' I am always tempted to ask, 'Compared to what?'

Sydney J. Harris (1917-)
Newspaper columnist

The greatest use of life is to spend it for something that will outlast it.

William James (1842-1910)
American psychologist and philosopher

Life begets life. Energy creates energy. It is by spending oneself that one becomes rich.

Sarah Bernhardt (1844-1923)
French actress

Each player must accept the cards life deals him. But once they are in hand, he alone must decide how to play the cards in order to win the game.

Voltaire (1694-1778)
French author

Life is not the way it's supposed to be. It's the way it is. The way you cope with it is what makes the difference.

Anonymous

I have a simple philosophy. Fill what's empty. Empty what's full. And scratch where it itches.

Alice Roosevelt Longworth (1884-1980)
Daughter of American President Theodore Roosevelt

The first rule in opera is the first rule in life: see to everything yourself.

Dame Nellie Melba (1865-1931)
Australian opera singer

There is no cure for birth and death, save to enjoy the interval.

George Santayana (1863-1952)
Spanish-American philosopher and poet

The main fact of life for me is love or its absence. Whether life is worth living depends on whether there is love in life.

R.D. Laing (1927-)
Scottish psychiatrist

You must understand the whole of life, not just one little part of it. That is why you must read, that is why you must look at the skies, that is why you must sing and dance, and write poems, and suffer; and understand, for all that is life.

Jiddu Krishnamurti (1895-1986)
Indian theosophist

When you were born, you cried and the world rejoiced. Live your life in such a manner that when you die the world cries and you rejoice.

Traditional Indian saying

Life can only be understood backwards; but it must be lived forwards.

Soren Aaby Kierkegaard (1813-1855)
Danish philosopher and theologian

Live all you can; it's a mistake not to. It doesn't so much matter what you do in particular, so long as you have had your life. If you haven't had that, what have you had?

Henry James (1843-1916)
American novelist

These, then, are my last words to you: be not afraid of life. Believe that life is worth living, and your belief will help create the fact.

William James (1842-1910)
American psychologist and philosopher

We love life, not because we are used to living,
but because we are used to loving.

Friedrich Wilhelm Nietzsche (1844-1900)
German philosopher, poet and scholar

The more we live by our intellect, the less we
understand the meaning of life.

Leo Tolstoy (1828-1910)
Russian writer

Children FEEL life. They smell it, roll in it, run
with it, see it all around them. Feel the world
through the eyes of a child.

Anonymous

Life is not made up of great sacrifices and duties
but of little things: in which smiles and kindness
given habitually are what win and preserve the
heart and secure comfort.

Sir Humphry Davy (1778-1829)
English chemist and poet

I want to be thoroughly used up when I die...Life is no brief candle to me. It's a sort of splendid torch which I've got to hold up for the moment and I want to make it burn as brightly as possible before handing it on to future generations.

George Bernard Shaw (1856-1950)
Irish dramatist, essayist and critic

I like life. I have sometimes been wildly, despairingly, acutely miserable, racked with sorrow, but through it all I still know quite cer-tainly that just to be alive is a grand thing.

Agatha Christie (1890-1976)
English mystery writer

Life was meant to be lived. Curiosity must be kept alive...One must never, for whatever reason, turn his back on life.

Eleanor Roosevelt (1884-1962)
First Lady of the United States, 1933-1945

— LONELINESS —

Pray that your loneliness may spur you into
finding something to live for, great enough
to die for.

Dag Hammerskjold (1905-1961)
Swedish diplomat

No man is lonely while eating a bowl
of spaghetti.

Sign in a spaghetti bar

That is part of the beauty of all literature. You
discover that your longings are universal
longings, that you're not lonely and isolated from
anyone. You belong.

F. Scott Fitzgerald (1896-1940)
American novelist

— LOVE —

The rule for us all is perfectly simple. Do not waste time bothering whether you 'love' your neighbour; act as if you did. As soon as we do this we find one of the great secrets. When you are behaving as if you loved someone, you will presently come to love him.

C.S. Lewis (1898-1963)
Irish-born academic, writer and poet

The only thing I know about love is that love is all there is...Love can do all but raise the dead.

Emily Dickinson (1830-1886)
American poet

Let us not be satisfied with just giving money. Money is not enough, money can be got, but they need your hearts to love them. So, spread love everywhere you go: first of all in your own home. Give love to your children, to your wife or husband, to a next-door neighbour.

Mother Teresa of Calcutta (1910-)
Yugoslav-born missionary

To love means never to be afraid of the windstorms of life: should you shield the canyons from the windstorms you would never see the true beauty of their carvings.

Elisabeth Kubler-Ross (1926-)
Swiss-born American psychiatrist

Him that I love, I wish to be free — even from me.

Anne Morrow Lindbergh (1906-)
American writer and aviator

Love is a fruit in season at all times, and within the reach of every hand. Anyone may gather it and no limit is set. Everyone can reach this love through meditation, spirit of prayer, and sacrifice, by an intense inner life.

Mother Teresa of Calcutta (1910-)
Yugoslav-born missionary

Love means to commit oneself without
guarantee, to give oneself completely in the
hope that our love will produce love in the loved
person. Love is an act of faith, and whoever
is of little faith is of little love.

Erich Fromm (1900-1980)
German-American psychoanalyst

I will greet this day with love in my heart. And
how will I do this? Henceforth will I look on all
things with love and I will be born again. I will
love the sun for it warms my bones; yet I will love
the rain for it cleanses my spirit. I will love the
light for it shows me the way; yet I will love the
darkness for it shows me the stars. I will welcome
happiness for it enlarges my heart; yet I will
endure sadness for it opens my soul. I will acknowledge rewards for they are my due; yet I
will welcome obstacles for they are my challenge.

Og Mandino (1923-)
American author

Love seems the swiftest, but it is the slowest of all growths. No man or woman really knows what perfect love is until they have been married for a quarter of a century.

Mark Twain (1835-1910)
American writer and humorist

Love is like quicksilver in the hand.
Leave the fingers open and it stays.
Clutch it, and it darts away.

Dorothy Parker (1893-1967)
American writer and satirist

Love consists in this, that two solitudes protect and touch and greet each other.

Rainer Maria Rilke (1875-1926)
Austrian poet

Love is, above all, the gift of oneself.

Jean Anouilh (1910-1987)
French dramatist

Love does not consist in gazing at each other but in looking together in the same direction.

Antoine de Saint-Exupery (1900-1944)
French airman and author

By love serve one another.

Galatians 5:13

Treasure the love you receive above all. It will survive long after your gold and good health have vanished.

Og Mandino (1923-)
American author

Men and women are made to love each other. It's only by loving each other that they can achieve anything.

Christina Stead (1902-1983)
Australian writer

I know of only one duty, and that is to love.

Albert Camus (1913-1960)
French writer

God doesn't look at how much we do, but with how much love we do it.

Mother Teresa of Calcutta (1910-)
Yugoslav-born missionary

Love is the free exercise of choice. Two people love each other only when they are quite capable of living without each other but choose to live with each other.

M. Scott Peck (1936-)
American psychiatrist and writer

The heart has reasons which the reason
cannot understand.

Blaise Pascal (1623-1662)
French physicist, theologian and writer

Love gives naught but itself and takes naught but
from itself. Love possesses not nor would it be
possessed; for love is sufficient unto love.

Khalil Gibran (1883-1931)
Lebanese poet, writer, artist and mystic

I define love thus: the will to extend oneself for
the purpose of nurturing one's own or another's
spiritual growth.

M. Scott Peck (1936-)
American psychiatrist and writer

— LUCK —

Anyone who does not know how to make the
most of his luck has no right to complain if it
passes him by.

Miguel de Cervantes (1547-1616)
Spanish author

I am a great believer in luck, and I find the
harder I work the more I have of it.

Stephen Leacock (1869-1944)
English-born Canadian economist and humorist

Luck to me is something else. Hard work — and
realising what is opportunity and what isn't.

Lucille Ball (1911-1989)
American actress

M

— MARRIAGE —

A happy marriage has in it all the pleasures of a
friendship, all the enjoyments of sense and
reason, and indeed, all the sweets of life.

Joseph Addison (1672-1719)
English essayist and politician

There is no more lovely, friendly, and charming
relationship, communion, or company than a
good marriage.

Martin Luther (1483-1544)
German religious reformer

Let there be spaces in your togetherness.

Kahlil Gibran (1883-1931)
Lebanese poet, writer, artist and mystic

Chains do not hold a marriage together. It is
threads, hundreds of tiny threads which sew
people together through the years. That is what
makes a marriage last — more than passion or
even sex.

Simone Signoret (1921-1985)
French actress

Give your hearts, but not into each
other's keeping,
For only the hand of life can contain your hearts.
And stand together yet not too near together:
For the pillars of the temple stand apart,
And the oak tree and the cypress grow not in
each other's shadow.

Kahlil Gibran (1883-1931)
Lebanese poet, artist and mystic

Two things do prolong thy life.
A quiet heart and a loving wife.

Anonymous

— MIND —

One man who has a mind and knows it can always beat ten men who haven't and don't.

George Bernard Shaw (1856-1950)
Irish dramatist, essayist and critic

Luck favours the mind that is prepared.

Louis Pasteur (1822-1895)
French bacteriologist

When people will not weed their own minds, they are apt to be overrun with nettles.

Horace Walpole (1717-1797)
English writer

The mind of man is capable of anything — because everything is in it, all the past as well as the future.

Joseph Conrad (1857-1924)
English novelist

The greater part of our happiness or misery depends on our dispositions and not on our circumstances. We carry the seeds of the one or the other about with us in our minds wherever we go.

Martha Washington (1731-1802)
First Lady of the United States, 1789-1799

The mind is its own place, and in itself
Can make a heaven of hell, a hell of heaven.

John Milton (1606-1674)
English poet

— MIRACLES —

Miracles happen to those who believe in them.

Bernhard Berenson (1865-1959)
American art critic

The miracle is not to fly in the air, or to walk on
the water; but to walk on the earth.

Chinese proverb

Where there is great love, there are
always miracles.

Willa Cather (1873-1947)
American writer

A miracle is an event which creates faith. Frauds
deceive. An event which creates faith does not
deceive; therefore it is not a fraud, but a miracle.

George Bernard Shaw (1856-1950)
Irish dramatist, playwright and critic

Everything is miraculous. It is a miracle that one
does not melt in one's bath.

Pablo Picasso (1881-1973)
Spanish painter

Why, who makes much of a miracle?
As to me I known nothing else but miracles —
To me every hour of night and day is a miracle,
Every cubic inch of space a miracle.

Walt Whitman (1819-1891)
American poet

The miracles of nature are all around us.

Anonymous

— MISERY —

Human misery must somewhere have a stop;
There is no wind that always blows a storm.

Euripides (480-406 BC)
Greek dramatist

The secret of being miserable is to have leisure to
bother about whether you are happy or not.

George Bernard Shaw (1856-1950)
Irish dramatist and critic

One often calms one's grief by recounting it.

Pierre Cornelle (1606-1684)
French dramatist

Who going through the vale of misery use it for a
well; and the pools are filled with water. They go
from strength to strength.

Psalm 84:6-7

— MISTAKES —

I have learned more from my mistakes than from
my successes.

Sir Humphry Davy (1778-1829)
English chemist and poet

Nothing would be done at all if a man waited
until he could do it so well that no-one could
find fault with it.

Cardinal John Henry Newman (1801-1890)
English theologian

The greatest mistake you can make in life is to be
continually fearing you will make one.

Elbert Hubbard (1856-1915)
American writer

There's nothing wrong in making a mistake — as
long as you don't follow it up with encores.

Anonymous

It is the greatest of all mistakes to do nothing
because you can only do little.

Sydney Smith (1771-1845)
English essayist, clergyman and wit

It has taken me thirty-three years and a bang on
the head to get my values right.

Stirling Moss (1929-)
English racing driver

If you have made mistakes...there is always
another chance for you...you may have a fresh
start any moment you choose, for this thing we
call 'failure' is not the falling down, but the
staying down.

Mary Pickford (1893-1979)
American actress

Some of the best lessons we ever learn, we learn
from our mistakes and failures. The error of the
past is the success and wisdom of the future.

Tyron Edwards (1809-1894)
American theologian

He who never made a mistake never made
a discovery.

Samuel Smiles (1812-1904)
Scottish author and social reformer

The man who makes no mistakes does not
usually make anything.

Edward John Phelps (1822-1900)
American lawyer and diplomat

A man should never be ashamed to own he has
been in the wrong, which is but saying, in other
words, that he is wiser today than he
was yesterday.

Alexander Pope (1688-1744)
English poet

Every great mistake has a halfway moment, a split second when it can be recalled and perhaps remedied.

Pearl S. Buck (1892-1973)
American writer

There are no mistakes, no coincidences; all events are blessings given to us to learn from. There is no need to go to India or anywhere else to find peace. You will find that deep place of silence right in your room, your garden or even your bathtub.

Elisabeth Kubler-Ross (1926-)
Swiss-born American psychiatrist

A life spent making mistakes is not only more honourable but more useful than a life spent doing nothing.

George Bernard Shaw (1856-1950)
Irish dramatist, essayist and critic

— MONEY —

The shortest and best way to make your fortune
is to let people see clearly that it is in their
interests to promote yours.

Jean de la Bruyere (1645-1696)
French satirist

Money, it turned out, was exactly like sex: you
thought of nothing else if you didn't have it and
thought of other things if you did.

James Baldwin (1924-1987)
American writer

Money is like an arm or leg — use it or lose it.

Henry Ford (1863-1947)
American motor car manufacturer

Money can't buy friends, but you can get a better
class of enemy.

Spike Milligan (1918-)
English comedian

If money is your hope for independence you will never have it. The only real security that a man can have in this world is a reserve of knowledge, experience and ability.

Henry Ford (1863-1947)
American motor car manufacturer

Money makes money, and the money money makes, makes more money.

Benjamin Franklin (1706-1790)
American statesman and philosopher

Money is like muck, not good except to be spread.

Francis Bacon (1561-1626)
English philosopher

— MUSIC —

I think I should have no other mortal wants, if I could always have plenty of music. It seems to infuse strength into my limbs and ideas into my brain. Life seems to go on without effort, when I am filled with music.

George Eliot (Mary Ann Evans) (1819-1880)
English novelist

Music is the medicine of the troubled mind.

Walter Haddon (1516-1537)
English writer

He who hears music feels his solitude peopled at once.

Robert Browning (1812-1889)
English poet

N

— NATURE —

There can be no very black misery to him who
lives in the midst of Nature and has his
senses still.

Henry David Thoreau (1817~1862)
American essayist, poet and mystic

Every part of this Earth is sacred to my people.
Every shining pine needle, every sandy shore,
every mist in the dark woods, every clearing and
humming insect is holy in the memory and
experience of my people

Chief Seathl
*From a letter written in 1883 to the President of the
United States.*

— NEGATIVITY —

Every day is irreplaceable, so don't ruin yours by
allowing the negative moods of others to pull you
into their frame of mind.

Anonymous

Try to avoid pessimists — negativity can
be catching.

Anonymous

Don't be too self-critical. Learn to be
on your own side.

Anonymous

— NEGOTIATION —

Let us never negotiate out of fear, but let us never
fear to negotiate.

John F. Kennedy (1917-1963)
President of the United States, 1961-1963

O

— *OCCUPATION* —

When men are rightly occupied, then
amusement grows out of the work as the
colour-petals out of a fruitful flower; when they
are faithfully helpful and compassionate, all their
emotions become steady, deep, perpetual and
vivifying to the soul as the natural
pulse to the body.

John Ruskin (1819-1900)
English author and art critic

Good for the body is the work of the body, good
for the soul is the work of the soul, and good for
either the work of the other.

Henry David Thoreau (1817-1862)
American essayist, poet and mystic

— OPPORTUNITY —

One cannot step twice into the same river.

Heraclitus (c.540-c.480 BC)
Greek philosopher

✶

Problems are only opportunities in work clothes.

Henry John Kaiser (1882-1967)
American industrialist

✶

A wise man will make more opportunities than
he finds.

Francis Bacon (1561-1626)
English philosopher

✶

Do not wait for extraordinary circumstances to
do good; try to use ordinary situations.

Jean Paul Richter (1763-1825)
German novelist and humorist

Failure is only the opportunity to begin again
more intelligently.

Henry Ford (1863-1947)
American motor car manufacturer

If heaven drops a date, open your mouth.

Chinese proverb

In the middle of difficulty lies opportunity.

Albert Einstein (1879-1955)
German-born physicist

A diamond is a chunk of coal that made good
under pressure.

Anonymous

To improve the golden moment of opportunity, and catch the good that is within our reach, is the great art of life.

William James (1842-1910)
American psychologist and philosopher

Opportunities are usually disguised as hard work, so most people don't recognise them.

Ann Landers (1918-)
American journalist

The people who get on in this world are the people who get up and look for the circumstances they want, and, if they can't find them, make them.

George Bernard Shaw (1856-1950)
Irish dramatist, essayist and critic

— OPTIMISM —

When one door shuts, another opens.

Proverb

In the midst of winter, I finally learned there was
in me an invincible summer.

Albert Camus (1913-1960)
French writer

An optimist is a person who takes action, who
moves out ahead of the crowd.

Anonymous

The optimist proclaims we live in the best of all
possible worlds; and the pessimist fears this
is true.

James Cabell (1879-1958)
American novelist and journalist

No pessimist ever discovered the secrets of the stars, or sailed to an uncharted land, or opened a new heaven to the horizon of the spirit.

Helen Keller (1880-1968)
Deaf and blind American lecturer, writer and scholar

I count only the sunny hours.

Sundial inscription

As you make your way through life,
Let this ever be your goal,
Keep your eye upon the doughnut
And not upon the hole.

Anonymous

A pessimist sees a glass that's half empty. An optimist sees a glass that's half full.

Anonymous

Over the winter glaciers
I see the summer glow;
And through the wild-piled snowdrift
The warm rosebuds below.

Ralph Waldo Emerson (1803-1882)
American essayist, poet and philosopher

To look up and not down,
To look forward and not back,
To look out and not in —
To lend a hand!

Edward Everett Hale (1882-1909)
American Unitarian clergyman and inspirational writer

An optimist sees an opportunity in every
calamity. A pessimist sees a calamity in
every opportunity.

Anonymous

— ORDER —

Order is the sanity of the mind, the health of the
body, the peace of the city, the serenity
of the state.

Chinese proverb

As the beams to a house, as the bones to the body
— so is order to all things.

Robert Southey (1774-1843)
English poet

Order is heaven's first law.

Alexander Pope (1688-1744)
English poet

A place for everything, and everything in
its place.

Samuel Smiles (1812-1904)
Scottish author and social reformer

— ORGANISATION —

Organisation is always the cornerstone of
business success.

Anonymous

A well-spent day brings happy sleep.

Leonardo da Vinci (1452-1519)
Italian painter, sculptor, architect and inventor

I must create a system, or be enslaved by
another man's.

William Blake (1757-1827)
English poet

Let all things be done decently and in order.

Corinthians 14:40

— ORIGINALITY —

What is originality? It is being one's self, and
reporting accurately what we see.

Ralph Waldo Emerson (1803-1882)
American essayist, poet and philosopher

All good things which exist are the fruits
of originality.

John Stuart Mill (1806-1873)
English philosopher

The dogmas of the quiet past are inadequate to
the stormy present. The occasion is piled high
with difficulty, and we must rise to the occasion.
As our case is new, so must we think anew and
act anew.

Abraham Lincoln (1809-1865)
President of the United States, 1860-1863

P

— PAIN —

The best way out of emotional pain is through it.

Anonymous

— PARTING —

Moments of kindness and reconciliation are
worth having, even if the parting has to come
sooner or later.

Alice Munro (1931-)
American writer

Weep if you must,
Parting is here —
But life goes on,
So sing as well.

Joyce Grenfell (1910-1979)
English comedian and writer

— PARENTHOOD —

Who of us is mature enough for offspring before the offspring themselves arrive? The value of marriage is not that adults produce children but that children produce adults.

Peter de Vries (1910-)
American novelist

Children are a bridge to heaven.

Anonymous

A mother is not a person to lean on but a person to make leaning unnecessary.

Dorothy Canfield Fisher (1879-1958)
American writer

One mother teaches more than a hundred teachers.

Jewish proverb

Love children especially, for, like angels, they too are sinless, and they live to soften and purify our hearts and, as it were, to guide us.

Feodor Dostoevsky (1821-1881)
Russian writer

Always believe in yourselves as parents. You are the best your children have.

Anonymous

Anything that parents have not learned from experience they can now learn from their children.

Anonymous

Children are likely to live up to what you believe of them.

Lady Bird Johnson (1912-)
First Lady of the United States, 1963-1969

— PAST —

The past exists only in memory, consequences,
effects. It has power over me only as I give it my
power. I can let go, release it, move freely, I am
not my past.

Anonymous

Even God cannot change the past.

Agathon (c. 446-401 BC)
Greek poet and playwright

Study the past, if you would divine the future.

Confucius (551-479 BC)
Chinese philosopher

— PATIENCE —

With time and patience the mulberry leaf
becomes a silk gown.

Chinese saying

Never cut what you can untie.

Joseph Joubert (1754-1824)
French writer

Patience is a bitter plant, but it has sweet fruit.

Proverb

There is nothing so bitter that a patient mind
cannot find some solace in it.

Lucius Annaeus Seneca (c.55 BC-c.40 AD)
Roman rhetorician

— PEACE —

Deep peace of the running wave to you.
Deep peace of the flowing air to you.
Deep peace of the quiet earth to you.
Deep peace of the shining stars to you.
Deep peace of the Son of Peace to you.

Celtic benediction

Do not be in a hurry to fill up an empty space
with words and embellishments, before it has
been filled with a deep interior peace.

Father Alexander Elchaninov
Russian priest

Do not lose your inward peace for anything
whatsoever, even if your whole world
seems upset.

Saint Francis de Sales (1567-1622)
French Roman Catholic bishop and writer

You will give yourself peace of mind if you per-
form every act of your life as if it were
your last.

Marcus Aurelius (121-180 AD)
Roman emperor and philosopher

Find peace within yourself by accepting not only
what you are, but what you are never
going to be.

Anonymous

Under this tree, where light and shade
Speckle the grass like a Thrush's breast,
Here in this green and quiet place
I give myself to peace and rest.
The peace of my contented mind,
That is to me a wealth untold —
When the Moon has no more silver left,
And the Sun's at the end of his gold.

W.H. Davies (1870-1940)
Welsh poet

— PERCEPTION —

If the doors of perception were cleansed,
everything would appear to man as it is, infinite.
For man has closed himself up, till he sees all
things through narrow chinks of his cavern.

William Blake (1757-1827)
English poet, artist and mystic

— PERSEVERANCE —

The drops of rain make a hole in the stone not by
violence but by oft falling.

Lucretius (96-55 BC)
Roman poet

God helps those who persevere.

The Koran

But what if I fail of my purpose here?
It is but to keep the nerves at strain,
To dry one's eyes and laugh at a fall,
And, baffled, get up and begin again.

Robert Browning (1812-1889)
English poet

Step by step the ladder is ascended.

George Herbert (1593-1633)
English poet

Consider the postage stamp; its usefulness
consists in the ability to stick to one thing
till it gets there.

Josh Billings (1818-1885)
American humorist

Finish whatever you begin, and experience the
triumph of completion.

Anonymous

Nothing in the world can take the place of persistence. Talent will not; nothing is more common than unsuccessful men with talent. Genius will not; unrewarded genius is almost a proverb. Education will not; the world is full of educated failures. Persistence and determination alone are omnipotent.

Calvin Coolidge (1872-1933)
President of the United States 1923-1929

To keep a lamp burning we have to keep putting oil in it.

Mother Teresa of Calcutta (1910-)
Yugoslav-born missionary

I have learned that success is to be measured not so much by the position one has reached in life as by the obstacles which one has overcome while trying to succeed.

Brooker T. Washington (1856-1915)
American black reformer

— PICK-ME-UPS —

It is almost impossible to remember how tragic a place the world is when one is playing golf.

Robert Lynd (1879-1949)
Irish essayist and journalist

★

There are a few things a hot bath won't cure, but I don't known many of them.

Sylvia Plath (1932-1963)
American poet and writer

★

Noble deeds and hot baths are the best cures for depression.

Dodie Smith (1896-1990)
English Writer

Where's the man could ease the heart
Like a satin gown?

Dorothy Parker (1893-1967)
American writer and satirist

Thank God for tea. What would the world do
without tea?

Sydney Smith (1771-1845)
English clergyman and essayist

Drink tea and forget the world's noises.

Chinese saying

A walk at dawn works wonders for the soul.

Anonymous

A little of what you fancy does you good.

English music hall song

— PLAN —

Plan your work and work your plan.

Norman Vincent Peale (1898-1993)
American writer and minister

Plan for the future because that's where you are
going to spend the rest of your life.

Mark Twain (1835-1910)
American writer and humorist

The time to repair the roof is when the sun
is shining.

John F. Kennedy (1917-1963)
President of the United States, 1961-1963

— PLEASURE —

One ought every day at least to hear a little song,
read a good poem, see a fine picture, and, if it
were possible, to speak a few reasonable words.

Johann Wolfgang von Goethe (1749-1832)
German poet, novelist and playwright

Life affords no higher pleasure than that of
surmounting difficulties, passing from one step of
success to another, forming new wishes and
seeing them gratified.

Samuel Johnson (1709-1784)
English lexicographer, critic and writer

The great pleasure of a dog is that you may make
a fool of yourself with him and not only will he
not scold you, but he will make a fool of
himself too.

Samuel Butler (1835-1902)
English writer

Only one hour in the normal day is more pleasurable than the hour spent in bed with a book before going to sleep, and that is the hour spent in bed with a book after being called in the morning.

Rose Macauley (1881-1958)
English novelist and essayist

Whenever you are sincerely pleased you are nourished.

Ralph Waldo Emerson (1803-1882)
American essayist, poet and philosopher

Pleasure for an hour, a bottle of wine; pleasure for a year, marriage; pleasure for a lifetime, a garden.

Chinese saying

— POSSIBILITY —

The only way to discover the limits of the possible is to go beyond them, to the impossible.

Arthur C. Clarke (1917-)
English science fiction writer

All things are possible until they are proved impossible — and even the impossible may only be so, as of now.

Pearl S. Buck (1892-1973)
American novelist

If I were to wish for anything, I should not wish for wealth and power, but for the passionate sense of the potential, for the eye which, ever young and ardent, sees the possible. Pleasure disappoints, possibility never.

Soren Kierkegaard (1813-1855)
Danish philosopher

— POTENTIAL —

Treat people as if they were what they ought to be and you help them to become what they are capable of being.

Johann Wolfgang von Goethe (1749-1832)
German poet, novelist and playwright

The greater the contrast, the greater the potential. Great energy only comes from a correspondingly great tension between opposites.

Carl Jung (1875-1961)
Swiss psychiatrist

To be what we are, and to become what we are capable of becoming is the only end of life.

Robert Louis Stevenson (1850-1894)
Scottish author and poet

— POVERTY —

The more you have, the more you are occupied,
the less you give. But the less you have, the more
free you are. Poverty for us is a freedom.

Mother Teresa of Calcutta (1910-)
Yugoslav-born missionary

— POWER —

Knowing others is intelligence; knowing yourself
is true wisdom.
Mastering others is strength; mastering yourself
is true power.

Lao-Tzu (c. 604 BC)
Chinese philosopher and founder of Taoism

I cannot do everything, but I can do something.
One person *can* make a difference.

Anonymous

— *PRAISE* —

I can live for two months on a good compliment.

Mark Twain (1835-1910)
American writer and humorist

Give credit where it's due.

Proverb

Once in a century a man may be ruined or made insufferable by praise. But surely once a minute something generous dies for want of it.

John Masefield (1878-1967)
English poet.

Some natures are too good to be spoiled
by praise.

Ralph Waldo Emerson (1803-1882)
American essayist, poet and philosopher

— PRAYER —

More things are wrought by prayer than this
world dreams of.

Alfred, Lord Tennyson (1809-1892)
English poet

Ask, and it shall be given to you; seek and ye shall
find; knock and it shall be opened to you.

Matthew 7:7

Teach me to feel another's woe,
To hide the fault I see,
That mercy I to others show,
That mercy show to me.

Alexander Pope (1788-1744)
English poet

When you prayest, rather let thy heart be
without words than thy words without heart.

John Bunyan (1628-1688)
English writer and moralist

You pray in your distress and in your need, would that you might also pray in the fullness of your joy and your days of abundance.

Kahlil Gibran (1883-1931)
Lebanese writer, artist and mystic

Prayer is not an old woman's idle amusement. Properly understood and applied it is the most potential instrument of action.

Mahatma Gandhi (1869-1948)
Indian leader., moral teacher and reformer

Oh Lord, help me
To be calm when things go wrong,
To persevere when things are difficult,
To be helpful to those in need,
And to be sympathetic to those whose
hearts are heavy.

Anonymous

— PRESENT JOYS —

Gather ye rosebuds while ye may,
Old time is still a-flying:
And this same flower that smiles today
Tomorrow will be dying.

Robert Herrick (1591-1674)
English poet

Ask not what tomorrow may bring, but count as
blessing every day that Fate allows you.

Horace (65-8 BC)
Roman poet

I try to make the here and now as heavenly as
possible, in case there isn't one to ascend into
when we're done. It's a kind of insurance.

Michael Caine (1933-)
English actor

— PROBLEMS —

First ask yourself, is this my problem? If it isn't,
leave it alone. If it is my problem, can I tackle it
now? Do so. If your problem could be settled by
an expert in some field, go quickly to him and
take his advice.

Dr Austen Riggs

I'm grateful for all my problems. As each of them
was overcome I became stronger and more able
to meet those yet to come. I grew on
my difficulties.

J.C. Penney (1875-1971)
American retailing magnate

I could do nothing without problems, they
toughen my mind. In fact I tell my assistants not
to bring me their successes for they weaken me;
but rather to bring me their problems, for they
strengthen me.

Charles Franklin Kettering (1876-1958)
American engineer and inventor

— PROCRASTINATION —

I have spent my days stringing and unstringing
my instrument, while the song I came to sing
remains unsung.

Rabindranath Tagore (1861-1941)
Indian poet and philosopher

Procrastination is the thief of time.

Edward Young (1683-1765)
English poet

Wasted days can never be recalled.

Anonymous

Q

— QUIET —

When you become quiet, it just dawns on you.

Thomas A. Edison (1847-1931)
American inventor

In the rush and noise of life, as you have
intervals, step home within yourselves and be
still. Wait upon God, and feel his good presence;
this will carry you evenly through your
day's business.

William Penn (1644-1718)
English Quaker and founder of Pennsylvania, USA

The good and the wise lead quiet lives.

Euipides (480-406 BC)
Greek dramatist

R

— RECEPTIVENESS —

Let us not therefore go hurrying about and collecting honey, bee-like, buzzing here and there impatiently from a knowledge of what is to be arrived at. But let us open out leaves like a flower, and be passive and receptive: budding patiently under the eye of Apollo and taking hints from every noble insect that favours us with a visit.

John Keats (1795-1821)
English poet

The rain falls on all the fields, but crops grow only in those that have been tilled and sown.

Chinese saying

— REGRET —

To regret one's own experiences is to arrest one's own development. To deny one's own experiences is to put a lie into the lips of one's own life. It is no less than a denial of the soul.

Oscar Wilde (1854-1900)
Irish poet, wit and dramatist

Make the most of your regrets...To regret deeply is to live afresh.

Henry David Thoreau (1817-1862)
American essayist, poet and mystic

What's gone and what's past help
Should be past grief.

William Shakespeare (1564-1616)
English playwright and poet

— RELATIONSHIP —

Only in relationship can you know yourself, not
in abstraction, and certainly not in isolation.

Jiddu Krishnamurti (1895-1986)
Indian theosophist

Once the realisation is accepted that even
between the closest human beings infinite
distances continue to exist, a wonderful living
side-by-side can grow up, if they succeed in
loving the distance between them, which makes it
possible for each to see the other whole
against a wide sky.

Rainer Maria Rilke (1875-1926)
Austrian poet

The worst sin towards our fellow creatures is not
to hate them, but to be indifferent to them; that's
the essence of inhumanity.

George Bernard Shaw (1856-1950)
Irish dramatist, essayist and critic

I do my thing, and you do your thing,
I am not in this world to live up to
your expectations
And you are not in this world to live up to mine.
You are you and I am I,
And if by chance we find each other,
it's beautiful.
If not, it can't be helped.

Frederick (Fritz) Salomon Perls (1893-1970)
German-born American psychologist

Personal relations are the important thing for
ever and ever, and not this outer life of telegrams
and anger.

E.M. Forster (1879-1970)
English novelist

I am a part of all that I have met.

Alfred, Lord Tennyson (1809-1892)
English poet

— RELIGION —

There is only one religion, though there are a hundred versions of it.

George Bernard Shaw (1856-1950)
Irish dramatist, essayist and critic

Be a good human being, a warm-hearted affectionate person. That is my fundamental belief. Having a sense of caring, a feeling of compassion will bring happiness or peace of mind to oneself and automatically create a positive atmosphere.

Dalai Lama (1935-)
Tibetan spiritual leader

Show love to all creatures and thou will be happy; for when thou lovest all things, thou lovest the Lord, for he is all in all.

Tulsi Das Hindu spiritual tradition

He who is filled with love is filled with
God himself.

St Augustine of Hippo (347-430 AD)

I consider myself a Hindu, Christian, Moslem,
Jew, Budhist and Confucian.

Mahatma Gandhi (1869-1948)
Indian leader, moral teacher and reformer

The worst moment for the atheist is when he is
really thankful, and has nobody to thank.

Dante Gabriel Rossetti (1828-1882)
English poet and painter

One man finds religion in his literature and
science; another finds it in his joy and his duty.

Joseph Joubert (1754-1824)
French writer

— REPUTATION —

The only time you realise you have a reputation
is when you fail to live up to it.

Anonymous

— RESILIENCE —

If you fell down yesterday, stand up today.

H.G. Wells (1866-1946)
English author

— REVOLUTION —

Revolution is the festival of the oppressed.

Germaine Greer (1939-)
Australian writer and feminist

— RIGHTEOUSNESS —

If there be righteousness in the heart, there will
be beauty in the character.
If there be beauty in the character, there will be
harmony in the home.
If there be harmony in the home, there will be
order in the nation.
If there be order in the nation, there will be
peace in the world.

Confucius (551-479 BC)
Chinese philosopher

I must stand with anybody that stands right,
stand with him while he is right, and part with
him when he goes wrong.

Abraham Lincoln (1809-1865)
President of the United States, 1861-1865

Right is might.

Anonymous

— RISK —

And the trouble is, if you don't risk anything, you
risk even more.

Erica Jong (1942-)
American novelist and poet

Don't refuse to go on an occasional wild goose
chase. That's what wild geese are for.

Anonymous

Risk! Risk anything! Care no more for the
opinions of others, for those voices. Do the
hardest thing on earth for you. Act for yourself.
Face the truth.

Katherine Mansfield (1888-1923)
New Zealand author

Risk is what separates the good part of life from
the tedium.

Jimmy Zero
American musician

S

— SAFETY —

The desire for safety stands against every great
and noble enterprise.

Publius Cornelius Tacitus (55-120 AD)
Roman historian

It is always safe to learn, even from our enemies;
seldom safe to venture to instruct, even
our friends.

Charles Caleb Colton (1780-1832)
English clergyman and author

The only way to be absolutely safe is never to try
anything for the first time.

Magnus Pyke (1908-)
English scientist

— SELF-CONFIDENCE —

Self-confidence is the first requisite to great undertakings.

Samuel Johnson (1709-1784)
English lexicographer, critic and writer

Self-trust is the first secret of success.

Ralph Waldo Emerson (1803-1882)
American poet and essayist

Those who believe they are exclusively in the right are generally those who achieve something.

Aldous Huxley (1894-1963)
English novelist and essayist

You can get good fish and chips at the Savoy; and you can put up with fancy people once you understand that you don't have to be like them.

Gracie Fields (1888-1979)
English singer

— SELF-CONTROL —

Just as a bicycle chain may be too tight, so may one's carefulness and conscientiousness be so tense as to hinder the running of one's mind.

William James (1842-1910)
American psychologist and philosopher

If your aim is control, it must be self-control first. If your aim is management, it must be self-management first.

Anonymous

Self-command is the main elegance.

Ralph Waldo Emerson (1803-1882)
American essayist, poet and philosopher

— SELF-DISCOVERY —

Learn to get in touch with the silence within
yourself and know that everything in this life has
a purpose.

Elisabeth Kubler-Ross (1926 -)
Swiss-born American psychiatrist

Just trust yourself, then you will know how
to live.

Johann Wolfgang von Goethe (1749-1832)
German poet, novelist and playwright

Once read thy own breast right,
And thou hast done with fears!
Man gets no other light,
Search he a thousand years.

Matthew Arnold (1822-1888)
English poet and critic

Pearls lie not on the seashore. If thou desirest one thou must dive for it.

Chinese proverb

In meditation it is possible to dive deeper into the mind to a place where there is no disturbance and there is absolute solitude. It is at this point in the profound stillness that the sound of the mind can be heard.

A.E.I. Falconar (1926-)
Indian-born philosopher

There is only one journey. Going inside yourself.

Rainer Maria Rilke (1875-1926)
Austrian poet

No one remains quite what he was, once he recognizes himself.

Thomas Mann (1875-1955)
German novelist

— SELFLESSNESS —

To give and not to count the cost;
To fight and not to heed the wounds;
To toil and not to seek for rest;
To labour and not ask for any reward
Save that of knowing that we do Thy will.

St Ignatius Loyola (1491-1556)
Spanish priest

Where self exists, God is not;
Where God exists there is no self.

Sikh morning prayer

Inwardness, mildness and self-renouncement do
make for man's happiness.

Matthew Arnold (1822-1888)
English poet and critic

— SELF-RESPECT —

Let us not forget that a man can never get away from himself.

Johann Wolfgang von Goethe (1749-1832)
German poet, novelist and playwright

No-one can make you feel inferior without your consent.

Eleanor Roosevelt (1884-1962)
First Lady of the United States, 1933-1945

It is difficult to make a man miserable while he feels he is worthy of himself.

Abraham Lincoln (1809-1865)
President of the United States of America, 1861-1865

If you put a small value upon yourself, rest assured that the world will not raise it.

Anonymous

A man cannot be comfortable without his own approval.

Mark Twain (1835-1910)
American writer and humorist

I think somehow we learn who we really are and then live with that decision.

Eleanor Roosevelt (1884-1961)
First Lady of the United States, 1933-1945

Self-respecting people do not care to peep at their reflections in unexpected mirrors, or to see themselves as others see them.

Logan Pearsall Smith (1865-1946)
English writer

— SILENCE —

Well-timed silence hath more eloquence
than speech.

Martin Farquhar Tupper (1810-1889)
English writer

— SINCERITY —

What comes from the heart, goes to the heart.

Samuel Taylor Coleridge (1772-1834)
English poet

What's a man's first duty? The answer's brief: to
be himself.

Henrik Ibsen (1828-1906)
Norwegian dramatist

— SMILE —

It takes seventy-two muscles to frown, but only thirteen to smile.

Anonymous

Smile at each other; smile at your wife, smile at your husband, smile at your children, smile at each other — it doesn't matter who it is — and that will help you to grow up in greater love for each other.

Mother Teresa of Calcutta (1910-)
Yugoslav-born missionary

A smile breaks down most barriers.

Anonymous

— SOLITUDE —

He who does not enjoy solitude will not love freedom.

Artur Schopenhauer (1788-1860)
German philosopher

I had three chairs in my house; one for solitude, two for friendship, three for society.

Henry David Thoreau (1817-1862)
American essayist, poet and mystic

Solitude is as needful to the imagination as society is wholesome for the character.

James Russell Lowell (1819-1891)
American poet, essayist and diplomat

Solitary trees, if they grow at all, grow strong.

Sir Winston Churchill (1874-1965)
English statesman

O Solitude, the soul's best friend,
That man acquainted with himself dost make.

Charles Cotton (1630-1687)
English poet

Go cherish your soul; expel companions; set your
habits to a life of solitude; then will the faculties
rise fair and full within.

Ralph Waldo Emerson (1803-1882)
American essayist, poet and philosopher

Living in solitude till the fullness of time, I still
kept the dew of my youth and the freshness of
my heart.

Nathaniel Hawthorne (1804-1864)
American novelist and short story writer

I never found the companion that was so
companionable as solitude.

Henry David Thoreau (1817-1862)
American essayist, poet and mystic

I am sure of this, that by going much alone, a man will get more of a noble courage in thought and word than from all the wisdom that is in books.

Ralph Waldo Emerson (1803-1882)
American essayist, poet and philosopher

Solitude is the nurse of enthusiasm, and enthusiasm is the true parent of genius.

Isaac D'Israeli (1766-1848)
English literary critic

— SOLUTION —

Every problem contains the seeds of its own solution.

Anonymous

— SORROW —

Truly, it is in the darkness that one finds the light,
so when we are in sorrow, then this light is
nearest of all to us.

Johannes Eckhart (c.1260-1327)
German mystic

★

One often calms one's grief by recounting it.

Pierre Corneille (1606-1684)
French dramatist

★

Pure and complete sorrow is as impossible as
pure and complete joy.

Leo Tolstoy (1828-1910)
Russian novelist

★

Blessed are they that mourn, for they shall
be comforted.

Matthew 5:4

— STRENGTH —

You must be the anvil or the hammer.

Johann Wolfgang von Goethe (1749-1832)
German poet, novelist and playwright

Be strong and courageous, and do the work.

Chronicles 28:20

The world breaks everyone and afterwards many
are strong at the broken places.

Ernest Hemingway (1899-1961)
American novelist

You who perceive yourself as weak and frail,
with futile hopes and devastated dreams, born
but to die, to weep and suffer pain, hear this: all
power is given unto you in earth and heaven.
There is nothing you cannot do.

A Course in Miracles

— STRUGGLE —

It seems to me that one of the greatest stumbling blocks in life is this constant struggle to reach, to achieve, to acquire.

Jiddu Krishnamurti (1895-1986)
Indian theosophist

Better that we should die fighting than be outraged and dishonoured...Better to die than live in slavery.

Emmeline Pankhurst (1858-1928)
Suffragette leader

The struggle that is not joyous is the wrong struggle. The joy of the struggle is not hedonism and hilarity, but the sense of purpose, achievement and dignity which is the reflowering of etiolated energy.

Germaine Greer (1939-)
Australian writer and feminist

Resistance to tyrants is obedience to God.

Benjamin Franklin (1706-1790)
American statesman and philosopher

Our greatest glory is not in never falling, but in rising every time we fall.

Confucius (551-479 BC)
Chinese philosopher

If a man lives without inner struggle, if everything happens in him without opposition...he will remain such as he is.

G.I. Gurdjieff (1877-1949)
Russian mystic and teacher of the occult

Golf without bunkers and hazards would be lame. So would life.

B.C. Forbes (1880-1954)
American writer

— SUCCESS —

Singleness of purpose is one of the chief
essentials for success in life, no matter what
may be one's aim.

John D. Rockefeller, Jr. (1874-1960)
American oil millionaire and philanthropist

I never allow any difficulties. The great secret of
being useful and successful is to admit
no difficulties.

Sir George Gipps (1791-1847)
Governor of New South Wales, 1838-1846

If one advances confidently in the direction of his
dreams, and endeavours to live the life which he
had imagined, he will meet with a success
unexpected in common hours.

Henry David Thoreau (1817-1862)
American essayist, poet and mystic

Success consists of getting up just one more time than you fall.

Anonymous

The only place where success comes before work is a dictionary.

Vidal Sassoon (1928-)
English hair stylist

A lot of successful people are risk-takers. Unless you're willing to do that...to have a go, fail miserably, and have another go, success won't happen.

Phillip Adams (1939-)
Australian author, writer and radio broadcaster

The secret of success is making your vocation your vacation.

Mark Twain (1835-1910)
American writer and humorist

There is only one success — to be able to spend your life in your own way.

Christopher Darlington Morley (1890-1957)
American novelist and essayist

If you want to succeed you should strike out on new paths, rather than travel the worn paths of accepted success.

John D. Rockefeller (1839-1937)
American oil millionaire monopolist and philanthropist

Success is to be measured not so much by the position one has reached in life, as by the obstacles which one has overcome while trying to succeed.

Booker Taliaferro Washington (1856-1915)
American teacher, writer and speaker

There are no gains without pains.

Adlai Stevenson (1900-1965)
American statesman

Do what you love and believe in, and success will
come naturally.

Anonymous

I cannot give you the formula for success, but I
can give you the formula for failure —
which is: try to please everybody.

Herbert Bayard Swope (1882-1958)
American newspaper editor

The toughest thing about success is that you've
got to keep on being a success.

Irving Berlin (1888-1989)
American composer

What's money? A man is a success if he gets up in the morning and goes to bed at night and in between does what he wants to do.

Bob Dylan (1941-)
American singer and songwriter

I've never sought success in order to get fame and money; it's the talent and the passion that count in success.

Ingrid Bergman (1915-1982)
Swedish-born actress

Getting ahead in a difficult profession requires avid faith in yourself. You must be able to sustain yourself against staggering blows and unfair reversals.

Sophia Loren (1934-)
Italian actress

The door to success has two signs,
Push — and Pull.

Leo Rosten's Treasury of Jewish Quotations

It is no good saying 'we are doing our best.' You
have got to succeed in doing what is necessary.

Winston Churchill (1874-1965)
English statesman

What is success?
To laugh often and much;
To win the respect of intelligent people and the
affection of children;
To earn the appreciation of honest critics and
endure the betrayal of false friends;
To appreciate beauty;
To find the best in others;
To leave the world a bit better, whether by a
healthy child, a garden patch or a redeemed
social condition;
To know even one life has breathed easier
because you have lived;
This is to have succeeded.

Ralph Waldo Emerson (1803-1882)
American essayist, poet and philosopher

— SUFFERING —

My personal trials have taught me the value of
unmerited suffering. As my sufferings mounted I
soon realised that there were two ways that I
could respond to my situation: either to react
with bitterness or seek to transform the suffering
into a creative force.

Martin Luther King (1929-1968)
American black civil-rights leader

— SUPERIORITY —

There is nothing noble about being superior to
some other man. The true nobility lies in being
superior to your previous self.

Hindu proverb

T

— TALENT —

Everyone has talent. What is rare is the courage
to follow the talent to the dark place where
it leads.

Erica Jong (1942-)
American novelist and poet

All our talents increase in the using, and every
faculty, both good and bad, strengthen
by exercise.

Anne Brontë (1820-1849)
English writer and poet

Conciseness is the sister of talent.

Anton Chekhov (1860-1904)
Russian writer

— TALK —

Who is there that can make muddy water clear?
But if allowed to remain still, it will gradually
become clear of itself...Be sparing of speech, and
things will come right of themselves.

Lao-Tzu (c. 604 BC)
Chinese philosopher and founder of Taoism

I don't care how much a man talks, if he only
says it in a few words.

Josh Billings (1818-1885)
American humorist

Talking and eloquence are not the same: to
speak, and to speak well, are two things.

Ben Jonson (1573-1637)
English dramatist

When you have nothing to say, say nothing.

Charles Caleb Colton (1780-1832)
English clergyman, sportsman, gambler and author

To talk is our chief business in this world, and talk is by far the most accessible pleasure. It costs nothing in money; it is all profit, it completes education, founds and fosters friendships, and can be enjoyed at any age and in almost any state of health.

Robert Louis Stevenson (1850-1894)
Scottish novelist, poet and essayist

The fact that people are born with two eyes and two ears but only one tongue suggests that they ought to look and listen twice as much as they speak.

Anonymous

— TEACHING —

It is the supreme art of the teacher to awaken joy
in creative expression and knowledge.

Albert Einstein (1879-1955)
German-born physicist

— TEARS —

The soul would have no rainbow
Had the eyes no tears.

John Vance Cheney (1848-1922)
American poet

The liquid drops of tears that you have shed
Shall come again, transform'd to orient pearl,
Advantaging their loan with interest
Of ten times double gain of happiness.

William Shakespeare (1564-1616)
English playwright and poet

— THANKS —

When you arise in the morning
Give thanks for the morning light.
Give thanks for your life and strength.
Give thanks for your food
And give thanks for the joy of living.
And if perchance you see no reason for
giving thanks,
Rest assured the fault is in yourself.

American Indian saying

Myself in constant good health, and in a
handsome and thriving condition. Blessed be
Almighty God for it.

Samuel Pepys (1633-1703)
English diarist

— THOUGHTS —

You may believe that you are responsible for what you do, but not for what you think. The truth is that you are responsible for what you think, because it is only at this level that you can exercise choice. What you do comes from what you think.

A Course in Miracles

A man is what he thinks about all day long.

Ralph Waldo Emerson (1803-1882)
American essayist, poet and philosopher

Every thought you have makes up some segment of the world you see. It is with your thoughts, then, that we must work, if your perception of the world is to be changed.

A Course in Miracles

The most immutable barrier in nature is between
one man's thoughts and another's.

William James (1842-1910)
American psychologist and philosopher

Thinking is the hardest work there is, which is
probably why so few engage in it.

Henry Ford (1863-1947)
American motor car manufacturer

Mind is everything; we become what we think.

Buddha (5th century BC)
Founder of Buddhism

The mind is never right but when it is at peace
within itself.

Seneca (4 BC-65 AD)
Roman philosopher and statesman

A great many people think they are thinking
when they are merely rearranging
their prejudices.

William James (1842-1910)
American psychologist and philosopher

Every revolution was first a thought in one
man's mind.

Ralph Waldo Emerson (1803-1882)
American essayist, poet and philosopher

Life does not consist mainly — or even largely —
of facts and happenings. It consists mainly of the
storm of thoughts that are forever blowing
through one's mind.

Mark Twain (1835-1910)
American writer and humorist

— TIME —

Don't serve time, make time serve you.

Willie Sutton (1860-1928)
American educationist

Dost thou love life? Then do not squander time;
for that's the stuff life is made of.

Benjamin Franklin (1706-1790)
American statesman and philosopher

Your time may be limited, but your imagination
is not.

Anonymous

These trying times are the good old days we'll be
longing for in a few years.

José Ferrer (1909-1992)
American actor

There is a time to be born, and a time to die, says
Solomon, and it is a memento of a truly wise
man; but there is an interval of infinte
importance between these two times.

Leigh Richmond (1772-1827)
English writer

Take time to think...it is the source of power.
Take time to play...it is the secret of
perpetual youth.
Take time to read...it is the fountain of wisdom.
Take time to pray...it is the greatest power
on earth.
Take time to laugh...it is the music of the soul.
Take time to give...it is too short a day to
be selfish.

Anonymous

It is familiarity with life that makes time speed quickly. When every day is a step into the unknown, as for children, the days are long with the gathering of experience.

George Robert Gissing (1857-1903)
English novelist

Lose an hour in the morning and you will be all day hunting for it.

Richard Whately (1787-1863)
English Archbishop of Dublin

You have to live on this twenty-four hours of daily time. Out of it you have to spin health, pleasure, money, content, respect and the evolution of your immortal soul. Its right use, its most effective use, is a matter of the highest urgency and of the most thrilling actuality. All depends on that. We shall never have any more time.

Arnold Bennett (1867-1931)
English novelist

Time goes, you say? Ah no! Alas,
Time stays, *we* go.

Henry Austin Dobson (1840-1921)
English poet

Let us spend one day as deliberately as nature,
and not be thrown off the track by every nutshell
and mosquito's wing that falls on the rails. Let us
rise early and fast, or break fast, gently and
without perturbation; let company come and let
company go, let the bells ring and the children
cry — determined to make a day of it. If the
engine whistles, let it whistle till it is hoarse for
its pains. If the bell rings, why should we run?
Time is but the stream I go a-fishing in.

Henry David Thoreau (1817-1862)
American essayist and poet

Time is what we want most, but what, alas, we
use worst.

William Penn (1644-1718)
English Quaker and founder of Pennsylvania, USA

An inch of gold will not buy an inch of time.

Chinese proverb

If only I could stand on a street corner with my hat in my hand, and get people to throw their wasted time into it!

Bernard Berenson (1865-1959)
American art critic

The future is something which everyone reaches at the rate of sixty minutes an hour, whatever he does, whoever he is.

C.S. Lewis (1898-1963)
Irish-born academic, writer and poet

We have to make the most of every secondo.

David Helfgott (1947-)
Australian concert pianist

Time is
Too slow for those who wait,
Too swift for those who fear,
Too long for those who grieve,
Too short for those who rejoice,
But for those who love, time is
Eternity. Hours fly, flowers die,
New days, new ways, pass by.
Love stays.

Sundial inscription

The busier you are, the more you find time to do
— and vice versa.

Anonymous

Our todays and yesterdays are the blocks with
which we build.

Henry Wadsworth Longfellow (1807-1882)
American poet

— TODAY & TOMORROW —

Look to this day...In it lies all the realities and
verities of existence, the bliss of growth, the
splendour of action, the glory of power. For
yesterday is but a dream and tomorrow is only a
vision. But today, well-lived, makes every
yesterday a dream of happiness and every
tomorrow a vision of hope.

Sanskrit proverb

Happy the man, and happy he alone,
He who can call today his own:
He who, secure within, can say
Tomorrow do thy worst, for I have lived today.

John Dryden (1631-1700)
English poet

Don't start living tomorrow — tomorrow never
arrives. Start working on your dreams and
ambitions today.

Anonymous

The bud of a rose is just as beautiful as the full
bloom. Appreciate what you have at
the moment.

Anonymous

Carpe diem. (Seize the day.)

Horace (65–8 BC)
Roman poet

It's only when we truly know and understand
that we have a limited time on earth — and that
we have no way of knowing when our time is up
— that we will begin to live each day to the
fullest, as if it was the only one we had.

Elisabeth Kubler-Ross (1926–)
Swiss-born American psychiatrist

What's lost today may be won tomorrow.

Miguel de Cervantes (1547–1616)
Spanish writer

After all, tomorrow is another day.

Margaret Mitchell (1900-1949)
American novelist

There is left for myself but one day in the week
— today. Any man can fight the battles of
today...It isn't the experiences of today that drives
men mad. It is the remorse for something that
happened yesterday, and the dread of what
tomorrow may disclose.

Robert J. Burdette (1844-1914)
American humorist

One today is worth two tomorrows; never leave
that till tomorrow which you can do today.

Benjamin Franklin (1706-1790)
American statesman and philosopher

— TOLERANCE —

Tolerance not only saves others from your prejudices and fears, but frees your soul to explore and accept the world that has been given to you.

Anonymous

Give to every other human being every right that you claim for yourself.

Robert G. Ingersoll (1833-1899)
American lawyer and orator

— TRANSFORMATION —

The meeting of two personalities is like the contact of two chemical substances: if there is any reaction, both are transformed.

Carl Jung (1875-1961)
Swiss psychiatrist

— *TRAVEL* —

Travel is fatal to prejudice, bigotry, and
narrow-mindedness.

Mark Twain (1835-1910)
American writer and humorist

Travel and change of place impart new vigour
to the mind.

Seneca (4 BC-65 AD)
Roman philosopher

Everyone's travels through life end the same way,
so you might as well enjoy the journey.

Anonymous

The soul of a journey is liberty, perfect liberty, to
think, feel, do just as one pleases.

William Hazlitt (1778-1830)
English essayist

— TRUTH —

The truth hurts like a thorn at first; but in the
end it blossoms like a rose.

Samuel Ha-Nagid (c. 900)
Jewish scholar

Men stumble over the truth from time to time,
but most pick themselves up and hurry off as if
nothing happened.

Sir Winston Churchill (1874-1965)
English statesman

It takes two to speak the truth — one to speak,
and another to hear.

Henry David Thoreau (1817-1862)
American essayist, poet and mystic

Nothing gives us rest but the sincere search for
truth.

Blaise Pascal (1623-1662)
French physicist, theologian and writer

Rather than love, than money, than fame,
give me truth.

Henry David Thoreau (1817-1862)
American essayist, poet and mystic

If you do not tell the truth about yourself you
cannot tell it about other people.

Virginia Woolf (1882-1941)
English writer

Truth is within ourselves; it takes no rise
From outward things, whate'er you may believe.
There is an inmost centre in us all,
Where truth abides in fullness.

Robert Browning (1812-1889)
English poet

The man who speaks the truth is always at ease.

Persian proverb

The truth is cruel, but it can be loved and it makes free those who love it.

George Santayana (1863-1952)
Spanish philosopher, poet and novelist

It is good to know the truth and speak it, but it is better to talk of palm trees.

Chinese proverb

— *TRYING* —

Until you try, you don't know what you can't do.

Henry James (1843-1916)
American novelist

U

— UNDERSTANDING —

A single moment of understanding can flood a
whole life with meaning.

Anonymous

If one is master of one thing and understands one
thing well, one has at the same time insight into
and understanding of many things.

Vincent Van Gogh (1853-1890)
Dutch post-impressionist painter

— UNIQUE —

All cases are unique, and very similar to others.

T.S. Eliot (1888-1965)
American-born poet and dramatist

V

— VICTORY —

He...got the better of himself, and that's the best
kind of victory one can wish for.

Miguel de Cervantes (1547-1616)
Spanish author

— VIRTUE —

Virtue is never left to stand alone. He who has it
will have neighbours.

Confucius (551-479 BC)
Chinese philosopher

W

— WEALTH —

Lazy men are soon poor.

Proverb

Wealth is a good servant, but a bad master.

Anonymous

Be not penny-wise; riches have wings and
sometimes they fly away of themselves;
sometimes they must be sent flying to bring
in more.

Francis Bacon (1561-1626)
English philosopher

— WINNING —

An integral part of being a star is having the will
to win. All the champions have it.

Betty Cuthbert (1938-)
Australian Olympic gold-medal sprinter

Only a loser finds it impossible to accept a
temporary set-back. A winner asks why.

Ita Buttrose (1942-)
Media personality

You have to make more noise than anyone else,
you have to make yourself more obtrusive than
anyone else, you have to fill all the papers more
than anyone else, in fact you have to be there all
the time...if you are really going to get your
reform realised.

Emmeline Pankhurst (1858-1928)
Suffragette leader

— WISDOM —

Be wiser than other people if you can, but do not tell them so.

Earl of Chesterfield (1694-1773)
English statesman

True wisdom consists in knowing one's duty exactly. True piety in acting what one knows. To aim at more than this, is to run into endless mistakes.

Bishop Thomas Wilson (1663-1755)
English churchman

In seeking wisdom, the first step is silence, the second listening, the third remembering, the fourth practising, the fifth — teaching others.

Ibn Gabirol (Avicebron) (1020-c.1070)
Jewish poet and philosopher

Knowledge comes, but wisdom lingers.

Alfred, Lord Tennyson (1809-1892)
English poet

I don't think much of a man who is not wiser
today than he was yesterday.

Abraham Lincoln (1809-1865)
President of the United States, 1861-1865

A wise man hears one word and
understands two.

Jewish proverb

The foolish man wonders at the unusual, but the
wise man at the usual.

Ralph Waldo Emerson (1803-1882)
American essayist, poet and philosopher

Be with wise men and become wise.

Proverbs 13:20

The wisdom of the wise, and the experience of
the ages, may be preserved by quotations.

Isaac D'Israeli (1766-1848)
English literary critic

He who knows others is learned; he who knows
himself is wise.

Lao-Tze (c. 604 BC)
Chinese philosopher and founder of Taoism

It is the province of knowledge to speak and it is
the privilege of wisdom to listen.

Oliver Wendell Holmes (1809-1894)
American writer

Every man is a damn fool for at least five minutes
every day; wisdom consists in not exceeding
the limit.

Elbert Hubbard (1856-1915)
American writer

The price of wisdom is above rubies.

Job 28:18

Nine-tenths of wisdom is being wise in time

Theodore Roosevelt (1858-1919)
President of the United States, 1901-1912

It is characteristic of wisdom not to do
desperate things.

Henry David Thoreau (1817-1862)
American essayist, poet and mystic

— WORDS —

Try to say the very thing you really mean, the
whole of it, nothing more or less or other than
what you really mean. That is the whole art and
joy of words.

C.S. Lewis (1898-1963)
Irish-born academic, writer and poet.

Man does not live by words alone, despite the
fact that sometimes he has to eat them.

Broderick Crawford (1911-)
American actor

— WORK —

To my mind the best investment a young man starting out in business could possibly make is to give all his time, all his energies to work, just plain, hard work.

Charles M. Schwab (1862-1939)
American industrialist

The glory of a workman, still more of a master-workman, that he does his work well, ought to be his most precious possession; like the 'honour of a soldier', dearer to him than life.

Thomas Carlyle (1795-1881)
Scottish essayist, historian and philosopher

It is impossible to enjoy idling thoroughly unless one has plenty of work to do.

Jerome K. Jerome (1859-1927)
English playwright and humorist

Choose a job you love, and you will never have to work a day in your life.

Anonymous

What's really important in life? Sitting on the beach? Looking at television eight hours a day? I think we have to appreciate that we're alive for only a limited period of time, and we'll spend most of our lives working. That being the case, I believe one of the most important priorities is to do whatever we do as well as we can. We should take pride in that.

Victor Kermit Kiam (1926-)
American corporate executive

The force, the mass of character, mind, heart or soul that a man can put into any work, is the most important factor in that work.

A.P. Peabody (1811-1893)
American writer

The highest reward for man's toil is not what he gets for it but what he becomes by it.

John Ruskin (1819-1900)
English writer and art critic

Whatsoever thy hand findeth to do, do it with thy might.

Ecclesiastes

Work is love made visible.

Kahlil Gibran (1883-1931)
Lebanese poet, author, artist and mystic

Nothing is really work unless you would rather be doing something else.

J.M. Barrie (1860-1937)
Scottish novelist

In order that people may be happy in their work, these three things are needed: They must be fit for it. They must not do too much of it. And they must have a sense of success in it.

John Ruskin (1819-1900)
English writer and art critic

Well begun is half done.

Proverb

The more one works, the more willing one is to work.

Lord Chesterfield (1694-1773)
English statesman and author

It is work that gives flavour to life.

Henri-Frederic Amiel (1828-1881)
Swiss philosopher and critic

There is no substitute for hard work.

Thomas A. Edison (1847-1931)
American inventor

To generous souls, every task is noble.

Euripides (480-406 BC)
Greek dramatist

No race can prosper till it learns that there is as
much dignity in tilling a field as in writing
a poem.

Booker Taliaferro Washington (1856-1915)
American teacher; writer and speaker

— WORRY —

I've found that worry and irritation vanish into
thin air the moment I open my mind to the many
blessings I possess.

Dale Carnegie (1888-1955)
American author and lecturer

As a cure for worrying, work is better
than whisky.

Thomas A. Edison (1845-1931)
American inventor

I have spent most of my life worrying about
things that have never happened.

Mark Twain (1835-1910)
American writer and humorist

I am an old man and have had many troubles,
but most of them never happened.

Anonymous

You're only here for a short visit. Don't hurry. Don't worry. And be sure to smell the flowers along the way.

Walter C. Hagen (1892-1969)
American golfer

Worry is interest paid on trouble before it falls due.

William Inge (1860-1954)
English prelate and author

Worries go down better with soup than without.

Jewish proverb

Y

— YES —

Where we are free to act, we are free to refrain from acting, and where we are able to say no, we are also able to say yes.

Aristotle (384-322 BC)
Greek philosopher

Say yes to life.

Anonymous

For what has been — thanks!
For what shall be — yes!

Dag Hammarskjold (1905-1961)
Swedish diplomat

— YOU —

Always be a first-rate version of yourself, instead
of a second-rate version of somebody else.

Judy Garland (1922-1969)
American singer

You have to live with yourself, so it's important
that you are fit for yourself to know.

Anonymous

Don't compromise yourself. You are all
you've got.

Janis Joplin (1943-1970)
American singer and songwriter

If I try to be like him, who will be like me?

Jewish proverb

One person's definition of success is another's first step. Only you can rate your accomplishments, and find peace within yourself.

Anonymous

To be nobody but yourself — in a world which is doing its best, night and day, to make you everybody else — means to fight the hardest battle which any human being can fight, and never stop fighting.

e.e. cummings (1894-1962)
English poet

— YOUTH —

Youth is a disease that must be borne with patiently! Time, indeed, will cure it.

R.H. Benson (1871-1914)
English novelist

Z

— ZEAL —

Zeal without knowledge is fire without light.

Thomas Fuller (1608-1661)
English divine and historian

— Subject Index —